HERMANN HESSE

Hermann Hesse

MODERN GERMAN AUTHORS
New Series

EDITED BY R. W. LAST

VOLUME TWO

HERMANN HESSE

THE MAN WHO SOUGHT AND FOUND HIMSELF

by

WALTER SORELL

OSWALD WOLFF
London

MODERN GERMAN AUTHORS—New Series
ed. R. W. Last

Volume One: HEINRICH BÖLL—Withdrawal and Re-emergence
              by James H. Reid
Volume Two: HERMANN HESSE—The man who sought and found
              himself
              by Walter Sorell

ISBN cloth 0 85496 049 x
paper 0 85496 050 3

© 1974 Oswald Wolff (Publishers) Limited,
London W1M 6DR

MADE AND PRINTED IN GREAT BRITAIN BY
THE GARDEN CITY PRESS LIMITED
LETCHWORTH, HERTFORDSHIRE
SG6 1JS

CONTENTS

page

PART ONE

Hesse As a Culture Hero   11

Portrait of the Artist as a Young Man   14

Following the Voice of Life   31

The Perilous Bridge between Body and Mind   40

East and West   48

Postscript to his Life   54

PART TWO

A Fighter in Search of Eternal Truths   59

The Essayist   69

Hesse's Brand of Humour   83

Music, Nature and Painting   94

In the Light of Criticism   107

    Versified Diary Notes   107

    The Polarities and God   115

    Love and Mother   124

    The Long Journey into the 'Within'   132

My Meeting with Hermann Hesse   137

Select Bibliography   140

For Hilde,
the Friend from Berne

PART ONE

PART ONE

HESSE AS A CULTURE HERO

Hermann Hesse was little appreciated by the Anglo-Saxon world during his long life (1877–1962). In private talks he often expressed his disappointment at having found such a poor response in America and England where interest in his work was mainly confined to students of German literature in colleges and universities. Hesse has been one of the favourite writers on the European continent, and even in Japan, for many decades. English readers, however, did not take to him, and this in spite of the fact that he was awarded the Nobel Prize for Literature in 1964. And, even though he was honoured by many more awards which spread his fame, the English versions of his books—there were only a few and not well translated—remained mostly unread.

Since the 1920's the trend among the English men of letters has increasingly moved towards the sophisticated novel with a great deal of entertainment value from Virginia Woolf and Aldous Huxley to Angus Wilson and Muriel Spark. The American reader has been either hungry for factual information, or has been reared within the realistic school of fictional writing from Theodore Dreiser to Ernest Hemingway. There has been little understanding for the soul-searching inwardness of Hermann Hesse's somewhat ponderous style and mystic and philosophical themes, nor for his Romanticism which seemed alien to most people used to living in a hectic world.

All this changed suddenly with the generation that came of age in the 1960's. Of course, they were not the first to be captured by the poetry of this novelist who went into his own wilderness to seek and find himself, who visualised his profession as a priest views priesthood, and whose writings, with their complexities hidden behind a disarming simplicity, reflect man in conflict with himself and the world. To give counsel and consolation became second nature to Hesse. He often compared Jesus (it could also have been Confucius or Buddha) with the role of the poet, describing the poet as a seeker and confessor whose concepts move between the poles of Truth and Beauty. Thinking of his task as a poet, he felt 'I must help understand and master the world for others who seek, and if by no other means than that I convey to them the consolation that they are not alone.' How much he thought of the tasks and duties of a poet becomes obvious when he maintains that there would be no need for any poets in the world, if Christ's churches and priests would be as Christ himself was.

Since Hesse's writings were very personal and emotionally intense, while his philosophical stance remained somewhat cool, he evoked a feeling of trust in the struggling minds of the young. He found his first wide response when he published his story *Peter Camenzind* in 1904. And when the century moved into its first traumatic phase during and particularly after World War I, those who returned from the front and all those who were frightened by the total collapse of all the old values found solace with Hesse and his novel *Demian*.

For the third time a young generation felt a strong spiritual kinship with this strange figure wandering through life in an almost monastic detachment from reality. These were the young people in the late sixties who sensed Hesse's mystical attachment to nature, his hostility towards the emphasis on intellectualism, his dislike for the bourgeois world with its set patterns and practicalities.

They were disillusioned and frightened people. Like Hesse, they sought a way back to simplicity. Many of the young people—those living in America and England were the most numerous and vociferous—had the courage to say no to their overmechanised surroundings. They sought hope and aspired to find it in a better understanding of nature and love. They called themselves flower children and tried to escape into a colourful Romantic past. They were followed by the neo-flower people, the post-hippies.

Many of them learned about Hesse's struggle to free himself from his inner chaos and to find a oneness with fate, a oneness of being. They knew that this was all that mattered. They wanted to sit still, to meditate, to look into themselves. They tried to hide behind all kinds of costumes. Their songs were soft and sentimentally real, while their rock'n'roll music could drown out reality. They found a whole new world in Woodstock. But they also walked barefoot or in sandals through the world, with a bag thrown over their shoulders and unkempt hair to such far-flung places as Morocco or even Nepal. They went to the East, embracing its wisdom and its timelessness. They were on their way to find themselves and a new meaning in life when they met and discovered Hermann Hesse. Listening to him, they understood that they were not alone.

PORTRAIT OF THE ARTIST AS A
YOUNG MAN

Since Hesse's thoughts returned to his childhood years and youth time and again, more space must be given to them in sketching his life and career than to any other subsequent phase. In many of his novels, essays, and letters the memory of those early years often light up as a luminous thought, as if in passing. In *The Steppenwolf* he suddenly remembers : 'My childhood and my mother showed in a tender transfiguration like a distant glimpse over mountains into the fathomless blue.' In his old age he loved to 'thumb through the picture book' of his life and jotted down odd bits of remembrances or mused about those early times in his *Rundbriefe*. When he had reached his seventy-fifth year, he wrote how much 'an object can mean' to old people 'speaking to them like a witness to the reality of their youth'. Hesse's entire work evokes the feeling of arrested moments of yesterday, and, among them, the memories of early life weigh most heavily.

We know a great deal about Hesse's grandfather on his paternal side because he wrote an autobiography for the benefit of his family. He married a girl who was very withdrawn, sickly and melancholy. Hesse's grandfather, however, was a strong man with a built-in gaiety, ready to accept all blows of fate as a devout believer in Jesus. From theology he turned to medicine overnight. He practised it all his life, even though he admitted in his diaries that most people did not think too highly of him as a physician. But he was undoubtedly very much liked for the person he was. Fate brought him to Estonia where he practised medicine and became a Russian citizen. One of his six children was a boy, called Johannes, who became the father of the poet-novelist-painter Hermann Hesse.

Hesse's mother was born in India. Her father, Dr. Hermann Gundert, came to India from Stuttgart where he had grown up in the religious atmosphere of the Bible Society. The young Gundert began his theological studies in the seminary of Maulbronn. He became intrigued by the more radical ideas of an awakening Germany—what we would call the New Left today—and wanted to leave the seminary in order to study history. He was enthusiastic about the July Revolution in Paris in 1830, dreamed of a new Poland and a free Germany.

Even though he was thrown into a spiritual crisis, torn between faith and free-thinking, he did not run away from the monastery as his grandchild did several decades later—but continued his theological studies at the Institute of Tübingen. But there, in 1833, a wave of suicides gripped the romantically inclined young and it was Hermann Gundert who succeeded in saving the life of his best friend. This was the moment in which he decided to become 'a missionary in India'.

Young Gundert heard of an important English family about to move there. The head of the family was looking for a tutor in Greek and Hebrew for his sons. And so Gundert went to England to join this family and expedition. He immediately plunged into an intense study of the idioms and grammar of Bengali and Hindustani. During the three months voyage to reach Madras, Gundert taught the Bengali language to all

15

those who had joined the expedition, among them also a certain Julie Dubois who came from Neuchâtel in Switzerland. Gundert remained close to a German mission already active near Madras. When one of the leading German missionaries died, a man to whom Gundert was very much attuned and who had wanted him to stay and work with his group, he asked for permission to leave the English family and join the brethren. This permission was granted, and it was then that he married Julie Dubois.

Dr. Gundert learned a new language, Malajalam, which turned into a lifelong study and love. His wife gave birth to four children, and one of them, Marie, became Hesse's mother. The children grew up in India, but after some adventurous years of preaching and teaching, Gundert fell sick, and the family returned to Europe. The Mission Society in Basle decided that Dr. Gundert had best join their publishing house in the small German town of Calw to which he moved with his family, his books, and his many treasures from India in order to complete his translation of the Bible into Malajalam.

Hermann Hesse's 'Indian' grandfather was a fascinating man whom Hesse beautifully described in *Childhood of the Magician* :

> This man, the father of my mother, hid in a forest of secrets as much as his face hid behind a wood of white beard; out of his eyes looked the grief of the world and serene wisdom, sometimes like the knowing of a lonely man, sometimes like divine drollery. People from many countries knew, revered and visited him, they spoke with him in English, French, Indian, Italian, Malayan and left again after their long conversations with him without leaving a trace behind them. Perhaps they were friends of his, perhaps his emissaries, perhaps his servants, deputies or proxies. From him, the

unfathomable, I surmised the secret which surrounded my mother, that age-old secret . . .

It was mere chance that made this high-spirited, thoroughly educated man, this gifted writer and linguist become a missionary. But are not all the chances we take or grasp in life somehow predestined? Such speculation is justified when we wish to speak of the background of Hermann Hesse. Life seems to be full of mysteries, and one of the greatest mysteries of all is always how two people find each other to unite and form the nucleus of another family while continuing the past whence they come. In short, how did Johannes Hesse, born in the cold north of Europe, meet and wed Marie Gundert, born under the burning sun of India?

While living through the icy Russian winters in his father's house, young Johannes Hesse perceived his father's struggle between his worldly attitudes and deeply religious feelings. The boy would spend hours in silence with God, as he said later, speaking with the Almighty about his father and his own worldly desires, hoping to find a way to serve a community that serves God. Johannes studied theology and one day wrote to the headquarters of the Missionary Society in Basle that he strongly felt the need 'to serve the Lord . . . in a practical way'. He was encouraged to become a missionary and later came to realise that this urge crystallised less from the wish to convert heathens than to bring sense and order into his own life and to educate himself properly.

After having worked in the Missionary School in Basle for some time, he went to Mangalur to preach in the seminary there. But the Indian climate had a bad effect on his health. The brethren called him back home and sent him as an assistant to the ageing Dr. Gundert in Calw. Johannes Hesse felt like a stranger in this medieval town. The only place in which he felt at ease was Dr. Gundert's house. Both men were united in their great love for India. He also soon developed a strong attachment for Marie. On 22 November 1874, the two were married.

Marie, Hermann Hesse's mother, was then in her thirties. The first four years of her life she had spent in India with her parents, but was sent to Europe for a proper education. This passionate, imaginative girl loved poetry and wrote a number of melancholy and Romantic poems herself. When she had reached her fifteenth year she was permitted to join her parents in India. She remained there for three years, helping her mother run the house and teach little Indian girls. She married a missionary, but after four years of a happy marriage her husband fell fatally ill. They had to rush back to Stuttgart where he died soon after their arrival. Four years later, left alone with two little boys, she met and married Johannes Hesse who was her senior by five years.

Marie no longer wrote poetry, but she never stopped writing diaries and letters with an almost compulsive need to note and annotate whatever happened in her daily life. So she wrote in her diary: 'On Monday 2 July 1877, after a difficult day God in His mercy gave us in the evening at half past six the long desired child, our Hermann, a very big, heavy, beautiful child that at once was hungry, with his bright blue eyes looking at the light, turning his head towards it all alone, a wonderful specimen of a healthy, strong boy. Today, on 20 July, I am writing this eighteen days later . . .'

From the very beginning Marie was aware of her

newborn son being somewhat different from any other child. She was quite in love with Adele to whom she had given birth two years previously. Adele seemed like an angel to her. 'There is something about her as if it were from Paradise,' she said (and our poet, too, was always very fond of his older sister). Hermann was an exceedingly friendly child, Marie felt, 'even while being seriously ill he often smiled at us', but there was something special and wilful about him.

For any mother it is one of the most gratifying feelings to see how quickly a child develops, how its cleverness augurs well for the future. In such cases most mothers tend to overlook or play down a child's less pleasant characteristics. Not Marie Hesse. She admitted from Hermann's second year on that, regardless of all his mental capacities, he seemed to be turning into a difficult boy. He was two and a half years old when she wrote in her diary:

> Little Hermann is developing pretty rapidly, he immediately recognises all pictures, whether they were from China, Africa or India, and he is very clever and entertaining, but his obstinacy and stubbornness are often highly amazing.

Both his bad temper and good mind worried his mother. She wrote in a letter:

> That boy is full of life, he is tremendously strong, has surprising willpower and really a stunning mind for his four years. Where will that lead to? It consumes my life's strength quite a bit, these inner struggles against his high-handed, tyrannical spirit.

In those days parents still thought the only way of correcting any wrongdoing of their children was by punishing them for the slightest misdemeanour. When, for instance, some time later Hermann played truant, his mother at once locked him in the guest room. Afterwards he told her: 'That doesn't help you much if you put me in there, I can look out of the window and have a good time.'

When Hermann was in his fifth year his father was called to Basle to take over the editorship of the Mission's magazine. The boy went to kindergarten and did rather well there. 'If only he would not have such a hot temper!' was his mother's constant refrain. At times his parents expressed satisfaction, and then it appeared to them that he was calming down and could more easily be guided. On other occasions he caused real despair. He was six when his father wrote:

> Hermann, who in school is considered a model of virtue, is sometimes insufferable. However humiliating it would be for us I seriously consider the possibility whether we should not send him to an institute or to strangers. We are too nervous, too weak for him, and our whole household is not sufficiently disciplined and regulated. He seems to be gifted for everything: he observes the moon and clouds, he can improvise on the harmonium for a long time, creates quite wonderful drawings with pencil and pen, can sing quite decently if he wants to, and it certainly never happens that he can't think of a rhyme.

There were several incidents of interest in Hermann's youth, and one or two of them may best characterise the conflicts and growing pains of those years. Quite early, to be exact on his fifth birthday, the boy rebelled against Fate, against all that makes us be the way we are, even though it was only a symbol against which he turned without quite knowing what he did.

After having played games with other children, games that ended in a fight, he attacked another boy called Arnold and then explained that one should not have given such a wicked boy this beautiful Biblical name. When his mother corrected him saying that the name of Arnold appeared nowhere in the Bible, Hermann maintained that he knew better. Then he talked about his own name which he found neither beautiful nor Biblical and concluded that his parents should have called him Seth. Adam and Eve called their good boy Seth whom God had given them as a token of solace for the dead Abel and the terribly wicked Cain. When little Hermann rebelled against having to live with his name he was not thinking of his Indian and Russian grand-fathers who were both called Hermann. We cannot know what made little Hermann dislike his name at that moment, if it was not a rebellious feeling against the name as a symbol, against having to live with something all his life on which his parents decided for him.

There is a very short note in Marie's diary on 11 November 1889: 'Hermann's theft of figs discovered.' This incident did not seem to mean much to his parents. To them it was one of many incidents that were a part of Hesse's process of growing up. It meant much to the boy because as a mature man he returned to the place of his crime, playing judge and healer while writing about a *Child's Soul*.

He told this story because its shadow fell across all the days of his life. He was in his twelfth year when it happened. On a Saturday morning he came home from school, and 'it was one of those days when fate lurks at all corners, when something could easily happen'. What happened was that the day had something dreary, boring and odious about it. Hesse described the feeling he then had: 'Damned and offensive was this life, it was full of lies and disgust. The grown-ups acted as if the world were perfect and if they themselves were demigods, we boys, however, nothing but dregs and scum. Those teachers—'

With this feeling he entered his home and felt many tempting demons lurking everywhere, 'huge and invisible, a spectre, a father and judge standing behind each wall'. Somehow he felt miserable and needed the touch of a familiar hand, some consolation. Since his mother was not in the living room he went up to his father's study. But no one was there either. The harmless visitor became an intruder, curiosity got hold of him, the playful thought of acting his father's role, or touching his things and of looking at them. He could feel his heart beat louder and faster. 'By no means did I then know what I would do. I only knew it would be something bad.'

The boy felt compelled to walk into the bedroom, when his 'father's image stood before me so clearly, reverence and rebellion fought in my heavy heart'. There was no reason for the boy to stay nor to open the closed drawers. But he stayed and looked into the drawers. He found figs in one of them and, without knowing what he did he filled his pockets with them, ran out and hid the figs in his room on his bookshelf.

He did not really care for figs, but he could not help doing something that was wrong. Pale in his face, he sat at the dinner table with his family and a bad conscience. His hands were hot as a thief's hands must be. In the afternoon he strolled around in town instead of going to school. When the school hours had passed he met a schoolmate on his way home and invited a fight, finally reaching his home with his shirt torn and bleeding. Entering he felt:

Oh God! It smelled of strictness, law and responsibility, of father and God. I stole. I was not a wounded hero who returned from a battle. I was not a poor child finding home and being put to bed by mother with warmth and compassion. I was a thief, I was a criminal.

Nobody had as yet noticed that the figs were missing. The many hours of waiting for the crime to be discovered were intolerable to him. The night was endless. Next day was Sunday. He went to church with his parents. And then, in the two hours between church and lunch, it happened.

Suddenly his father stood behind him. There were still a few of the figs behind the books. The cross-examination began. One lie led to the next. The boy claimed to have bought the figs at the grocer. Where did he take the money from? His father knew he would have to lie again. He made him walk with him to the grocer. It was Sunday. His father knew the store was closed. So they went to see the grocer at his home. His father knew the boy would have to confess before they entered the grocer's house.

Of course, he knew everything! And he kept me dancing, kept me executing my senseless caprioles as one makes a mouse dance, caught in its trap, before one drowns it. Oh, if at the very beginning he had only hit me with his cane over the head without questioning and interrogating me, I would have preferred it to all his calm and justice with which he caught me in the web of my stupid lies and slowly strangled me.

Then the reproaches followed. Why did he lie? If he only knew why he lied, if he only knew why he stole those figs!

Hesse explained that at that time he did not know what he knew today while writing this story of his youth. He stole because he came to his father in need of a

23

comforting look or word and was disappointed in finding the room empty. Then finding his father's desk intriguing, with the many books, manuscripts and letters lying around, he wanted to find something about the secret of his father's life. But there were only figs hidden in a drawer. He stole them. For a whole day and night the boy was tortured by what he had done and needed forgiveness. 'If I could have told him all that, he might have understood me. But also children, so superior to the grown-ups in their understanding, often stand in front of their fate lonesome and helpless.'

The story has its natural ending. The father would ask once more : 'Why did you steal the figs?', knowing that there was no answer to this question. And there was none. The boy was locked in the attic for the entire Sunday afternoon. In the evening before going to sleep his father talked to him. They were on good terms again. 'Lying in bed', the mature Hesse wrote about his feelings at that time, 'I was sure that he had forgiven me, wholly and completely—more completely than I forgave him.'

One more incident must be mentioned because it had serious and decisive consequences. In 1891, Hermann entered Maulbronn, a seminary, where he was supposed to be trained and educated for the career of a theologian and possibly a missionary as his own father and his mother's father were. Hermann has expressed his doubts about such a career, even before he went to Maulbronn. But his parents urged him to try it, and his father's voice could be heard : 'I tell you : you are in good hands with the Saviour. Try it with him.' Uncertain of himself, Hermann entered the seminary to please his parents.

In the beginning he adjusted to the life in school, to all its regimentations and was quite happy there.

Learning came easy to him, he especially loved Latin, but he utterly disliked mathematics and Hebrew. By and by the limitations in his personal freedom and the compulsion of having to learn so many things which seemed unnecessary and boring to him became more and more insufferable. Moreover, he was by then utterly convinced of having no inclination for being a pastor or missionary. It was then that he wrote many poems and felt happiest when he could write, and there was hardly an hour in which he would not write. As he said later : 'From my thirteenth year on one thing was clear to me. I wanted to become a poet or nothing at all.'

It also became soon apparent that he was little equipped to live a strictly regulated existence with so many other boys. He could not take a life in which every hour had its defined activity dominated by rules and regulations, in which every step was more or less a part of a precisely arranged community existence. No doubt, the value of comradeship and friendship became quite obvious to him. But his silent and dreamy nature and his inmost desire to be by himself stamped him as an outsider and rebel in the eyes of his teachers and of most of his schoolmates.

He had entered Maulbronn on 15 September 1891. Not quite six months later, on 7 March 1892, during the recess between two periods, Hermann had his books in his hands and mentioned to some of his schoolmates that he would walk out of the place. Nobody took him seriously. He, however, walked out of the seminary as if into the world, into freedom—as he was, with his books under his arm which he had prepared for the next lecture. He walked across the fields and through the woods, a 'wanton dreamer', as the boy later wrote his parents. He spent a freezing night on an open field, covering himself with the straw he found there. He walked around for twenty-three hours without a coat or gloves, without a coin in his pocket. The school sent out search parties into all directions and alarmed the police. The next day a dazed boy, freezing, trembling all over his body, passed a gendarme who asked him where he was going. When Hermann said, 'Maulbronn,' the officer went with him to make sure he would arrive there.

Since he had never complained about being at Maulbronn, his teachers took his escapade very seriously, treating him like a sick rather than wicked boy. They considered him mentally ill, at least disturbed, an outsider, not a rebel. Regulations had to be adhered to and detention for eight hours was to be his punishment, with only bread and water but all the books he cared to take along. It was Homer's *Odyssee* he took with him to keep him company.

Hermann Hesse was considered a menace to his schoolmates and, as the Principal expressed it, 'there always was a certain danger that his overstimulated imagination can easily overcome his willpower', and 'his unnatural and unhealthy thoughts and feelings' had to be watched. His parents accepted this verdict. They would have been even more ill at ease about his mental condition, had they bothered to read some of the poetry that poured out of him in those days. The day before his escape—Hermann wrote the date to most of the poems he jotted down in youthful exuberance and haste—he wrote a poem which was not important from a literary viewpoint, but very expressive and characteristic of the mood he was in. It was eight lines of deeply melancholy feeling, one of desperate aloneness of a sensitive boy struggling with the world and himself :

> Alone on the mountain slope,
> Alone with all my woe,
> My eyes along the heaven grope
> And look in the calm lake below.
>
> The lake is as blue as the sky.
> I felt within me naught but night,
> As if in the water I should die
> And all would be all right.

He loved music as much as poetry. He learned to play the violin in Maulbronn. He always looked for a silent place where he could play and play for himself. He knew he would never become a virtuoso. Moreover, this was not what he wanted. He wanted to be able to dream on his violin, not practise to compete with others and progress to please his teacher. An unpleasant encounter between the young Hesse and his music teacher occurred two days before his escape.

The year 1892, when he was not yet quite fifteen, was a time of awakening and confusion, of struggle against his parents and teachers, against pastors and physicians, against an entire world thinking in terms of practicalities and acting as if all life could be reduced to mere reality. Hermann had then begun to dream a great dream which never left him : the dream of a poet, and he fought valiantly against everyone and everything in his fear that the world was bent on killing his dream. (Did not Pastor Schall—who headed the sanatorium for mentally sick people in Stetten and in whose care Hermann was for several months—write to Hermann's father that he was doing everything in his power to make clear to the boy 'that one cannot exist in life with just playing the violin and writing poems'?)

Maulbronn became to him the symbol of a world demanding strict obedience, service and purpose in life in which his pious family believed (and, strangely enough, which he extolled in his last and crowning work, *The Glass Bead Game*, even though on another level and for a higher purpose). However, at that time he had to turn against it so that he could create the life he dreamed of, and in his stubbornness he went to extremes in defying those men who thought, in their righteousness, that they could speak for God. Everything in Hermann Hesse cried out for more than he found in Maulbronn, everything asked 'for a deliverance of his awakened longing or guidance through the riddles whose solution was too difficult for him to find'.

The after-effects of his escapade were severe. He fell sick, suffered from bad headaches, dizzy spells, and lost weight. He was brought home for a short time. Hesse wrote about this homecoming and how he most feared his grandfather whom he had to visit 'in order to accept his verdict and punishment. With my heart beating fast I walked up the staircase to his study, knocked at the door, entered and approached the bearded old man'. And what did the man say who was so feared and all-knowing?

> He looked at me in a friendly way, looked at my pale and frightened face, smiled at me with a glint in his eye and said: 'I was told, Hermann, you took the trip of a genius?' This was the phrase for such and similar escapades in the old man's student years. No further word was said in this matter.

Dr. Hermann Gundert may have remembered his own difficulties at Maulbronn. Children are always better understood by their grandparents than their parents. However this may be, this incident was the only bright moment in this dark period of Hesse's life. His parents vacillated between the belief that either Hermann was possessed by an evil spirit or perhaps mentally sick. The boy was first brought to Bad Boll where Pastor Christoph Blumhardt had the reputation of being a miracle doctor. Although Hermann went through happy days there in the beginning, even through the sweet experience of a first love and its disappointment, Blumhardt's exorcising and mesmerising methods only led to more nervous breakdowns, more crises, and a suicide attempt.

Still in the same year, Hermann was sent to Stetten where Pastor Schall tried to cure him. He kept him busy with physical work, mainly in the garden, with teaching and strict regulations. Again this failed. After a short stay in Basle Hermann sought to continue his studies in the junior college of Cannstatt. The year was 1893. He was sixteen years old, but his struggle with the world and himself went on. He still rebelled against and was at odds with those who stood for strict measures and enforced order. He still indulged in dreaming and writing poetry. He still suffered from headaches at times and felt weak. He passed one exam, but in the fall of that year he asked for permission to leave school. He wanted to work. Employment was found for him in a bookseller's in the town of Esslingen. But after two days of work he did not return to the shop. When he was found in Stuttgart a few days later, he was sick and very weak.

The next few months until June 1894 Hermann spent at home to recover, to find himself. Occasionally he helped his father in his office or worked in the garden. What he loved most was to sit in his grandfather's library among the many books on Asia, to look at the figures of Buddha and other images from a remote world. He read and wrote. When, later in life, he said about himself, 'at the age of fifteen I began consciously and energetically to educate myself', only then could he know how very true this statement was.

Shortly before June 1894 Hermann decided on turning a new page in his life. He wrote his father, with whom he lived under the same roof, a very long letter:

> ... I choose the circumstantial way of writing you ... I did not like it in the seminary, just as little in Cannstatt and Esslingen. You took it as a sign of sickness that I always ran away. Of course, it was not the right thing to do, but I had no inclination, no strength, no courage for all that you wanted to make of me ... My free hours I used to educate myself. You called it breadless art and so forth, but I hoped and hope I will be able to live on it. I never had the courage to tell you about my intentions and wishes, as I knew they would not correspond with yours. This is how we got further apart time and again ... Now a decision is necessary ...

On 5 June 1894, Hermann Hesse accepted employment as a mechanic in H. Perrot's workshop. A new phase began in Hesse's life.

FOLLOWING THE VOICE OF LIFE

Hesse entered H. Perrot's workshop as a mechanic, eager to break out of himself. Perrot produced clocks, and Hesse, who had a way of being faithful to his past, immortalised the name of Perrot in *The Glass Bead Game* as the inventor of the mechanics of this game. His own career as a mechanic was of short duration. At that time he dreamed and planned to emigrate to Brazil. But Brazil was only a symbol for another escape from the narrowness of life, a desire for more experiences and inner adventures. What he really wanted was to be with the reality of fiction, with books. One day he advertised in the *Stuttgarter Merkur* asking for work in a bookseller's. He was accepted by the Heckenhauer bookshop in Tübingen. He was then eighteen years old.

From clocks to books. Tübingen, a small, medieval town, created the environment Hesse needed and liked. His room consisted of nothing but books, the walls were filled with portraits of poets and composers which he cut out of catalogues and magazines. He worked for this bookshop for four years. He read and dreamed a great deal, but he also succeeded in learning the trade. He wrote as intensely as he read ('. . . In those years I made my first attempt at finding myself as a poet and I read half the world's literature, art history and philosophy . . .').

A small volume of poetry was followed by his first book of prose whose title was borrowed from one of his poems : *An Hour Behind Midnight*. One of his first reviewers wrote :

31

It is worthwhile talking about a book which, inspired by awe and piousness, speaks to us in a dark, praying voice: for art is piousness; piousness towards oneself, towards all experience, all things, towards a great image and one's own untested strength ... Out of such feelings Hermann Hesse's book emerged.

The reviewer's name was Rainer Maria Rilke.

Hesse was twenty-two years old when he left Tübingen and settled in Basle where he continued his apprenticeship at the bookseller's R. Reich, formerly C. Detloff. The man for whom he worked published his next book, nine poems and three pieces of prose: *Hermann Lauscher*. It is indicative of Hesse's serious difficulties with himself that he said later about this book: 'It was an attempt at conquering a piece of the world and reality and escaping the dangers of a partly diffident, partly arrogant lonesomeness.'

Judging from the first two books, it becomes obvious that Hesse was inclined to observe himself and account for all his actions with methodical exactitude. It was at this early stage of his career that a few salient features became noticeable which later on determined his entire life and work: a compulsive self-analysis and a narcissistic trend went hand in hand; his deep-rooted stubbornness led to a strong defence mechanism and helped separate the outer and inner world; his own experiences were visualised from two different angles and aspects, roles which Hesse played were distributed among two different characters, mostly friends and hidden antagonists.

Time and again Hesse came back to the memories of his past in an arbitrary manner. There was no chronological sequence in his return to things past, except perhaps the psychological need at certain periods of his life to hitch his thoughts to moments and experiences which he then could not shake off, as it seems.

In December 1899 he wrote to his friend Ludwig Finckh, 'You know I am here in Basle ... selling old, precious books. But I am about to write new ones which no one else has written yet.' A journey to Italy resulted in a few poems and articles for newspapers and magazines. The small fees added to his small salary as a bookseller. A modest income kept him going. At the age of twenty-five he rejected the offer of a much better paid position in a Leipzig museum dedicated to the technical aspects of book publishing. I mention this because of Hesse's reasoning. By then he had wandered through many parts of Switzerland and had come to feel at home in the cultural atmosphere of Basle. The advantages of a better and secure position meant nothing to him in comparison to 'the greater freedom and life in Switzerland which has become home for me'.

Towards the end of 1902 the Swiss writer Paul Ilg called the attention of the renowned German publisher, S. Fischer, to Hesse's potentialities as a poet-novelist. The publisher asked him to submit his next book. Hesse replied that

> my writings are purely personal attempts, intimate things expressed in a modern form, that, therefore, they hardly qualify to become considerable book successes, a fact I do not have to stress. I don't write very much and only out of very personal needs.

Such a purely personal account was his first major novel, *Peter Camenzind*, which was an immediate success when issued in 1904. It enabled him to live as a freelance writer from then on.

Peter Camenzind is a novelist's study in Romanticism.

33

In his mistrust of the world and its society, Hesse made *Camenzind* into a paean on nature, with a faint echo coming from Rousseau's sentimental rebellion. There are many passages, lyrically beautiful, extolling love and nature, the nature of love and the love for nature, in an almost puerile, mystic belief in the power of both. On the other hand, where doubt is cast on the petty ways of life in the city, on the empty gaiety of the intellectuals, Hesse's descriptions sound more like literature than life. Camenzind, a stranger in a bourgeois world, finally withdraws to a hermit existence at his mountain birthplace.

At the time of the Camenzind success Hesse married Maria Bernoulli and left Basle with her to live at the little place of Gaienhofen at Lake Constance. With his anti-bourgeois novel began Hesse's bourgeois life. It was a peasant house in which they lived, and for the first time he had a feeling of belonging, of having settled down, 'but from time to time also a feeling of being imprisoned, penned in by borders and order'. There were many moments in this happy, secure life when he asked himself : But am I really happy?

After three years he built his own house there, more spacious and with a garden which meant a great deal to him. This house where he lived until 1912 saw many visitors. Hesse befriended a number of musicians and painters at that time whose faces found their way into many of his novels. In this period of bourgeois existence he wrote many minor stories, articles, book critiques (he never chose to review a book he did not like!) because he needed the money. Of the novels then written the first one was *Under the Wheel* in which Hesse returned to the time of his student days. His own experiences are represented by two boys, one reflecting Hesse's escapade from the seminary, the other his serious adolescent

sufferings. Some of the unhappiness he experienced in
Gaienhofen found its way into the novel. Together with
his friend Finckh, Hesse often ran away from home to
angle, sail or catch butterflies as his student does. Hesse
remembered his own days of tribulations when he
depicted this student as a victim of ambitious educators,
including his father. In letting the student get under the
wheel, Hesse struck an accusing and fighting attitude
against the crushing of young spirits. This novel was not
quite as strong in its impact as *Peter Camenzind*, but—
perhaps because of its topic—was a best-selling book
for a long time.

Gertrud, written in 1910, is another novel of Hesse's
Gaienhofen period. In this book Hesse tried to escape
into the invisible realm of music where one could still
find some saving grace. Hesse saw little joy and redemption in life at that time. In his despair he could write
such truisms : 'Life was whimsical and cruel, there was
neither kindness nor reason in nature.' Both, reason and
kindness, could perhaps be found sporadically in a
human being, but then only for a short duration.

The narrator of this novel tells the story of the
musician Kuhn who, crippled through an accident, loses
the girl he loves to his friend and later, after the friend's
early death, remains close to her in silent love and
friendship. *Gertrud* is a badly constructed novel. For
the first time, Hesse, then very popular among German
readers, was widely and wildly attacked by the press.
He admitted that Gertrud as a character stood in the
background, was used as a symbol and mostly as a
stimulant for the musician Kuhn who needed her for
his development.

Gaienhofen too was only a symbol for him, a small
place somewhere on the map where he could escape the

noise, confusion and perplexities of civilisation. But even there he had run away from his own home to find the lonesomeness of his heart and his dream of nature. He read and wrote, lectured in many towns and edited a magazine. His three sons were born. (Psychologists may make a point of how he expressed it : 'In Gaienhofen I received my three sons.') His life was full of unfulfilled longing ('I am destined to follow the voice of life, even though I do not yet recognize meaning and goal . . . and even though this voice tries to lure me away from the street of gaiety and towards darkness and uncertainty').

When, in 1911, he journeyed to India it was an escape for the sake of escape. Perhaps he wanted to see with his own eyes what his mother saw and where she lived, to experience what he only knew from books. However, the dream images gained from the books lost their beauty when confronted with the reality that was India. He returned tired and disappointed. This mood is the undercurrent in his travelogue, *From India*. Even moments of experienced surprise were accompanied by little excitement, the darkness of night seemed so much darker there than in Europe, for which he longed while being in India. Much later, when the image of the real India became submerged in his poetic dream of the continent, one of his most beautiful books, *Siddhartha*, came into being. After his immediate return from the East, he left Gaienhofen with his family and settled in the outskirts of Berne, moving into the house of the late painter Albert Welti.

His stay there was destined to form a bridge into another phase of his life. The novels which were published in 1914 and 1915 were *Rosshalde* and *Knulp*. The outside and inward events were of cataclysmic intensity: the First World War, the serious disease of his wife, and his own nervous breakdown.

The feeling of aloneness and futility, already expressed in *Gertrud*, came to the fore with full force in *Rosshalde*. Johannes Veraguth, completely immersed in his work as a painter, is locked in a desperate struggle with his wife, completely immersed in music. The novel's drama is the sickness and death of their son Pierre, the trauma is the failure of the marriage. Hesse's unhappiness in his marriage is the problem with which he wrestles: Should any creative artist or thinker, who must live instinctively and create as objectively as possible, become involved in a marriage? Is he at all qualified to marry? Hesse wrote to his father: 'I do not know the answer to it, but my own feeling for it is expressed in the book as precisely as possible; I followed a thing there to its very end with which I hope to cope differently in life.' The fact that his wife had to be committed helped him to a somewhat happier end of an unhappy ending.

Knulp, published in 1915, seems, in retrospect, to be like a last farewell to a youthful period in Hesse's life that was about to have run its course. Knulp is the loveable vagabond with a child's soul, another dream image of Hesse as a vagabond himself. There is the joyful, carefree man juxtaposed with the homeless, lonesome fellow who decided to sell any ordered existence for the price of total freedom. It is insinuated that Knulp became a vagabond because of an unhappy love affair in his early youth. Did Hesse believe that the right woman can be *the* solution for man? He was inclined to say yes as often as no. Later, in *Demian*, he may have defined best what he meant: 'He had loved and found himself through love. Most of us, however, love to lose ourselves.'

37

With all his wanderlust and homesickness for an undefined world rather than a home, Knulp echoes the poetic charm and confusion of Josef Eichendorff's *Taugenichts*, that Good-for-Nothing, who enchanted an earlier Romantic period. But behind all the lightness in *Knulp* lies Hesse's wrestling with God and fate. Hesse, the seeker, thought that life is what we make of it. The errant vagabond cannot blame anyone else but himself for his existence and, looking at his final balance sheet, he hears the voice of God: 'Look here, I didn't want you to be different from what you are, and I had to impart to you that sting of homelessness and urge to wander, otherwise you might have stayed put somewhere and spoiled my game...' When Knulp, in his last moments of dialogue with God, resigns himself to the fact that he has nothing to complain about and everything is fine the way it has been, His voice says: 'Then you found home and you'll stay with me.'

Hesse felt that man's soul is his fate and is an invisible and infinitesimal piece of God. In His name Knulp roamed around to bring a bit of homesickness for freedom to the sedentary bourgeois people, as Hesse said. This is an interesting notion when we think of Hesse and the young people in the late sixties for whom the homesickness for freedom, some kind of undefinable freedom, was a strong impetus.

However resigned Hesse may have been to his own fate, the debacle of the entire civilisation, the loss of any feeling for decency and integrity among the best German writers of the time who had all joined the chorus of war cries, all depressed and infuriated him. He turned against the war psychosis with such essays as *O Friends, Not This Tone!* in which he spoke out against the nationalistic madness in 1914. He joined Romain

Rolland in his doomed effort to bring back reason and peace to man and incessantly worked for the prisoners of war. His father's death, his wife being committed, his youngest son, Martin, falling sick with a mental disease which made Hesse fear the worst, and the vilifications coming from across the border, from German journalists, poets as much as academicians who branded him as a traitor of the German cause—all these momentous elements combined to throw Hesse into deep depression.

His physician advised him to stop all activities and withdraw to the sanatorium Sonnmatt near Lucerne. There he began his long sessions, about sixty altogether, with the Jung disciple, Dr. J. B. Lang, who soon was to become Hesse's friend. They grappled with Hesse's mother fixation and general neurotic condition. These sessions were explorations of an imaginary world into which the poet had escaped. Two years later, in 1918, he wrote an essay, *Artist and Psychoanalysis*, in which he said :

> He who goes the way of analysis far enough will harvest lasting gain, a more intimate relationship to his own subconscious. He can experience a warmer, more productive and passionate interrelation between his consciousness and unconsciousness.

THE PERILOUS BRIDGE BETWEEN
BODY AND MIND

'The sickness seems to be gone,' Hesse wrote in 1919, 'I have not died. Once more earth and sun are turning for me.' It was the year when he, 'a burnt-out literati', left Berne and escaped to the south of Switzerland in his quest for solitude to find himself and re-establish his bankrupt life. His three sons were cared for by close friends. He knew that his marriage with Maria Bernoulli, even after her release from the asylum, was a closed chapter.

It was the year when he realised that 'he no longer enjoyed writing', and because of the writer's block he discovered the joy of painting. Hesse settled in Montagnola, then a small village above Lugano. The landscape of the Ticino seemed to have waited for the painter H.H. : to be loved, experienced and water-coloured. Painting, which he never gave up from then on, showed him the way back to writing.

It also was the year in which his novel *Demian* was published. This book was written so that no one should any longer feel he had to lie to himself, Hesse thought. There is a mystical quality in young Emil Sinclair's struggle with his daimon which he faces in his friend Max Demian, and with his dream image of the eternal mother and beloved whom he finds in Demian's mother. It is a dream-like, almost labyrinthine, path by which Sinclair finds himself. The process of Sinclair's self-education through friend and woman was Hesse's first successful journey into the hidden world within. Equating man's psyche with man's fate he could say : 'There is someone within me who knows everything.' The inner world of symbols became unravelled and exposed to the daylight of awareness. Hesse had gained new strength through his analysis and was able to put the mother image into a clearer perspective. He made Sinclair overcome and renounce his dependence on Mother Eva, finding self-realisation.

Demian was first published under the pseudonym of Emil Sinclair and received the Fontane Prize which Hesse returned when Eduard Korrodi, eidtor of *Die Neue Zürcher Zeitung*, revealed the real author. That Hesse should have chosen a pen name at this point of his life is symptomatic of his full awareness of *Demian* having been a total break with his past. He wanted to prove demonstratively to himself rather than to the world that a new H.H. had emerged.

At the time of Demian's publication, Hesse was in the Ticino, and the beginning in his new environment was one of his most creative periods. Two novellas, *Klingsor's Last Summer* and *Klein and Wagner* were written within a short time. *Klein and Wagner* is vaguely based on a *cause célèbre* of a psychopathic schoolteacher by the name of Ernst Wagner who murdered his wife and four children. It is more closely related to Hesse's former emotional needs to break away from his bourgeois ties.

Hesse pictured the clerk Friedrich Klein as a split personality who sees himself kill his family in his dream, embezzle money and escape into a new world of empty adventures. He changes his persona. In his visions the name of Wagner is identified with his teacher and his tormenting spirit, with the murderer Wagner whose deed he finds justified, and Richard Wagner, the idol of his youth. He struggles with his conflicting feelings during his little adventures, becomes involved in gambling, is attracted by a dancer, and one night when he wakes up next to her naked beauty, he is tempted to kill her and finally drowns himself. One of the key sentences of this story states that we live in the dark, never really live our own life, and this is what sickens man who will perish because of it.

During those early years in Montagnola he experimented with a simple way of life in an almost Thoreau-like fashion :

> I lived on milk and rice and macaroni, I wore my old suits until they fell apart, and in the autumn I brought my dinner home from the woods in the form of chestnuts. The experiment I tried out succeeded and, despite all the hardships of these years, they were beautiful and productive. As if I would awake from nightmares, nightmares which had lasted for years, I embraced freedom, the air, the sun, the feeling of being alone, my work.

This freedom gave his creative mood an ecstatic feeling. But writing and painting still meant to him working on himself, and what he had to say in those years was often clouded with past experiences and the vision of a dark tomorrow.

A feeling of apocalyptic doom hovers over *Klingsor's Last Summer*. There is a cry of exaltation reverberating throughout the story : 'We must perish, we must be reborn, the great turn has come for us.' Klingsor, the painter, groping for a solution in his creative struggle, hopes to find it in the consoling power of music, as Van Gogh knew before him. But the music is a music of decay. Hesse pictures him sitting in his burning house, singing, and it is he who puts his own house on fire.

Klingsor fears the end but is in love with his fear of death. He lives with the zest and fervour of raving mad wantonness, he cannot stop yearning to empty all cups, and this intensified living is little more but the fear of the end.

Klingsor knows all about our childish and futile gestures. He is an artist because he cannot help raging against that unknown moment that may be the final one. 'Our entire art,' we read, 'is merely a substitute, a troublesome and ten times too dearly paid for substitute for missed life, missed beastliness, missed love.' He misses none of it, and with his creations he wants to prove how strong and triumphant life can be in spite of the inevitable end. Klingsor is Romanticism personified. Klingsor's last summer has come. He will die, and we will learn that the time for such magicians has gone.

The figure of Klingsor was close to Hesse who was full of passionate, if not great, music in those days. Everything sounded as if colours could be heard to sing. On the other hand, everything lives in a world of deception: black and white are a deception as much as life and death or good and evil.

His next book, *Wandering*, contained rhymed verses and rhythmic prose, verbal frames for some of his watercolours. Hesse still reflected on his inner dissonances when, in the opening paean on his farewell to the northern landscape, he said :

I wanted to be a poet, but a burgher too. I wanted to be an artist and a man of imagination, but, at the same time, also to be virtuous and enjoy my home. It took me a long time before I knew that one can't have both.

Whenever Hesse has to say farewell to whatever it may be, it is as if he had to take leave of his mother.

Here it is the typical peasant house of the northern landscape, but:

> I say goodbye to you like a young man to his mother. He knows it is time for him to leave and he also knows that he will never be able to leave her altogether even if he wanted to.

This period was followed by one of soberness tinged with irony as if our poet-novelist had felt the need to fall from one extreme mood into another. Between the years of 1923 and 1930 his persona took on several new shades. Two events at that time were formal acts which did not seem to bring about any incisive changes. Almost in passing he married for the second time, but his marriage with Ruth Wenger was of short duration. It was of far greater significance that Hesse asked to become a Swiss citizen in 1923. Again, I should have said, since he was a Swiss as a child, but later when he attended German schools it was an act of convenience for him to become a German citizen. Hesse loathed nationalism and knew of no borders. However, when he realised that the Germans betrayed their hard-won democracy after World War I, Hesse felt the need to sever his formal relationship with this nation. Moreover, he had lived all his adult years in Switzerland.

If fate is something deep within one's soul, as Hesse believed, then these were ambivalent years during the twenties and corresponded with the rhythm of contrasts which all polarities and possibilities embraced. He could put on the mask of a Klingsor or Klein, Demian or Siddhartha. Despite the complexities of his life, analysing them in retrospect helped him gain an amazing awareness of his neurotic condition, a strength to laugh about it and to write psycho-autobiographically more consciously than ever before. The freedom he felt over his own difficulties widened the channels of humour and enabled him to glorify his inner struggles both literally and literarily. Only his visionary ability and the power to give poetic form to what he had to say, saved his work from being painfully personal. The documentation of his own experiences was skilfully veiled or defiantly presented as a reflection of his own time.

The two works that followed must be regarded as non-fictional if we do not wish to consider that Hesse could write about Hesse as a fictional character. He stayed in Baden for some time to cure his sciatica. As an observer of himself and the scene about him he wrote a strange book which he called *Guest at a Spa*. It functions on several levels as an analysis of the modern artist's neuroses as well as a whimsical report on the life at a spa. In his treatment symptoms became symbols, as Hugo Ball said, and Hesse's intentions have far-reaching connotations of a sick society not quite sure what ails it.

This book has a companion piece in his travelogue, *The Nuremberg Journey*, written on the occasion of a trip from Lugano to Nuremberg. The fascinating aspects of this report are the many asides and philosophically humorous speculations about everything only faintly related to the journey. If one word leads to the next, then certainly one thought makes another one emerge as if from nowhere. This report is filled with the wisdom of a man who knows how to use his cornucopia of ideas. He proves himself as a teller of tales who skilfully varies the pace from an experience to an anecdote, from a sudden notion to an observation that is apropos.

The Steppenwolf, one of Hesse's most popular novels, was written about that time. It is as disconcerting as it is powerful in its structure and in the strength with which it indicts an era of jazz and loud-mouthed lies, a sham world in which the sensibilities of man are tested and crucified. Like Hesse, the Steppenwolf is an outsider living on the edge of reality. Wrestling with his despair, groping for his innocence and his beliefs in a life of lost values, he seeks to find himself. His bearings are those of a bourgeois, but the stamp of his soul spells the anathema of the outsider. The city in which the novel's hero, Harry Haller, seems to be lost, is a symbol of unrelatedness. Someone puts a pamphlet into his hand, 'The Treatise on the Steppenwolf,' in which he finds the analysis of himself. There is his split nature, being man and wolf, kind and wild, full of love and tenderness as much as baring his wickedness and savagery. God and the Devil are in these people, 'the capacity for happiness and the capacity for suffering; and in just such a state of enmity and entanglement were the wolf and man in Harry'.

The problem for the Steppenwolf is to pacify and unify these two extremes in order to find contentment. But this is not only the problem of one man. Hesse tried to give form to the sickness of his time. He challenges man to walk through hell, chaos and the darkened world of man's soul. In this journey through life's hell Harry Haller fails the test, but he is shown the way through a magic theatre of the immortals. Theirs is a timeless world of faith in which the mind can triumph over chaos and barbarism. Hesse's prescription to believe in the laughter of the immortals and to unify the struggling forces through the intellect apparently can be applied only by the intellect. But does he not assume that he who suffers most is the thinking animal in man whose heightened sensibilities endanger him?

Three years later he treated the same theme once more

in *Narcissus and Goldmund*, but in a more palatable, Romantic mood for the average reader by placing the story in medieval days. The struggling forces are symbolised by the monk Narcissus who is all intellect, the spirit of asceticism, and Goldmund, who tries to explore and embrace the world of sensuousness and sensuality. Goldmund is the paragon of the creative artist whose eternal longing for the unfulfilled part of his being drives him from one adventure to another. This is a modern version of the Prodigal Son pitted against his brother, whose life is determined by constancy, work, and prayer. It certainly shows once more the split nature of one being, or the dichotomy of two worlds, the maternal and paternal spirits.

Goldmund cannot resist the temptations of the flesh, the adventures with the unknown. Hesse, the moralist, makes Goldmund realise that love is composed of lust and pain, and he makes the artist in Goldmund aware that the final accomplishment remains unfulfilled. Goldmund dies before completing what he considers his masterpiece, the great Eve-Mother. Through all his adventures in life Goldmund has tried to capture her enigmatic face. Only in his imagination can he see it. When trying to hold on to it, the hallowed image eludes him.

Both are defeated: Narcissus knows about suffering and sadness through the spiritual ecstasy of his solitude. He tries to find inner peace through his mind as Goldmund tries to find his in giving in to the ecstasy of his senses. Hermann Hesse captured his life's philosophy in *The Steppenwolf* and *Narcissus and Goldmund* with different actors in a different setting and mood. But it is the quintessence of his experiences and visions, even though he speaks to us through a variety of masks.

EAST AND WEST

Hesse was magically drawn to the East. No doubt, the seed was planted in his early youth. However, the feeling of lostness in the Western world with its stress on the ego, on action and the machine drove him eastward. Moreover, the introvert in him inclined towards contemplation, was attuned to Eastern philosophy.

However ambivalent his feelings were when he journeyed to India in 1911, his immediate reaction was a timid attempt to understand the reality of something whose ideation alone was of meaningfulness to him. He needed to be wedded spiritually to the East, not in real terms.

Three of his novels testify to this assumption. All three are unique and different in their way. It took him eleven years after his return from India to visualise *Siddhartha*. It took him another ten years to write *The Journey to the East*. It took him twenty-one more years to complete *The Glass Bead Game*. All three works represent the poeticised translation of his image of the East into his personal world, an amalgam of Protestant defiance and Taoistic passivity and simplicity.

Siddhartha is a man seeking the inner peace of completion. A contemporary of Buddha, he finds him and listens to him. His friend Govinda joins the Illustrious One, but Siddhartha shies away from doctrines and teachers. He feels, as Hesse always felt, that he must go alone to reach his goal. He cannot simply accept any ready-made formula which arouses his stubbornness. The Illustrious bidding him farewell warns Siddhartha : 'Be on your guard against too much cleverness.'

First, Siddhartha had to live the life of the world and senses before he could find himself, and he could find himself only through experiencing the inexpressible, the ultimate wisdom, the elemental spirit of all existence. The simile of the river and the insight of the simple ferryman Vasudeva who, in Siddhartha's eyes, becomes a tree, a god, an image of eternity, teaches him all that can be 'in harmony with the stream of events, with the stream of life, full of sympathy and compassion, surrendering himself to the stream, belonging to the unity of all things'.

Like Vasudeva, who found his oneness with the river, with the peaceful flow of the water that was, is and will be, Siddhartha realised that you can communicate knowledge, but not wisdom which everyone must gain through his own experiences. You can love things like the river, the stone, the tree. 'But one cannot love words.' It was, therefore, through silence and a kiss on Siddhartha's forehead that he communicated his inner experience of peace to his friend Govinda.

This book, written with poetic simplicity and the power of conviction, is a European's experience of the East. With Siddhartha there can no longer be any doubt that East and West met in Montagnola.

The Journey to the East was another attempt at reaching and embracing a timeless, non-geographic concept of unified existence. It is another journey in which departure and destination are as vaguely defined as our life which is only seemingly determined by both. Hesse's goal is again the realisation of the self. Neither space nor time exist on this journey whose goal 'was the home and youth of the soul, it was everywhere and nowhere, it was the union of all times'. H.H. often wandered with many, he says, sometimes with a few friends only or quite alone.

An irreplaceable document was taken along by the League of these Journeyers which disappeared with the servant Leo. But it is not certain whether it was taken along at all; it may have been only a copy. The document's importance, however, has never been in question since it holds the secret of existence of which we are aware without being able to spell it out, the magic of life and the power of experience. Leo who remained behind (like a steppenwolf) or deserted the group had carried the luggage. What is the luggage as a symbol of life if not the mental burdens we drag along? Leo's disappearance is a test for all of them. In appearance a servant, he was actually the leader, the one on whom everyone relied. Now that he had gone, the League seems to disintegrate, only its great idea still remains. Hesse holds on to the illusion of an ideal world which threatens to disappear, defying forgetfulness and failure. The archive of the League is still intact, and the archive symbolises the treasures of man's culture.

One of the messages of this book is to praise servitude and obedience, humility and faith. H.H. as self-accuser is summoned to a trial. Leo calls for him, turning out to be the President of the League passing judgment on H.H. The case was dismissed as 'novitiate stupidities'. Although H.H. was acquitted, his errors and negligence, his despairs and disbeliefs were stated. It was the conscience of H.H. that condemned him, but he paid his spiritual debts by trying to understand the secret of life and to justify his understanding of it. In a final scene H.H. realises that much of his being must disappear and give way to the substance he finds in Leo's image. With this realisation the curtain falls on this elusive mystery play.

The visualisations conveyed to us through *The Journey to the East* become reality in *The Glass Bead Game* which Hesse 'dedicated to the Journeyers to the East'. The world of Castalia which Hesse created was projected into an unspecified future, a world of order and measure, of awe and discipline pitted against the chaos of reality. As suggested in *The Journey to the East*, Hesse believed in the necessity of a spiritual hierarchy which must devote its attention to the education of an elite. He intended to juxtapose this ideal world with the real world of triumphant mediocrities, crude materialism and cultural bankruptcy at the 'Age of the Feuilleton'.

In Castalia the future elite is educated with the desire, as Hesse explains, for a 'unio mystica of all disparate elements of the Universitas litterarum'. It is an utterly esoteric approach to a world symbolising a temporally remote island in which the wisdom of East and West unites to create an ideal community of savants, with the spirits of Mozart and Lao Tse called upon to reign supreme.

This work should have been 'a mode of expression for stability in the midst of flux', as he said in a letter to Rudolf Pannwitz in 1955, 'for the continuity of tradition and the cultural life in general'. *The Glass Bead Game* was written in the years in which Nazism poisoned the German mind and threatened to destroy all culture. Therefore, we must see the genesis of this work as a protest against the Teutonic furore and the danger of the destruction of all spiritual values of the past. This is why Hesse could conclude the letter:

Two things were important for me: to build up a spiritual space in which I could breathe and live despite all poisoning of the world, a refuge and castle; secondly, I wanted to express the resistance of the mind against the barbarous powers and, if possible, to strengthen my friends in Germany in their resistance and perseverance.

In a few prefatory pages Hesse introduced the meaning of *The Glass Bead Game*:

The Glass Bead Game is thus a mode of playing with the total contents and values of our culture; it plays with them as, say, in the great age of the arts a painter might have played with the colours on the palette. All the insights, noble thoughts, and works of art that the human race has produced in its creative eras, all that subsequent periods of scholarly study have reduced to concepts and converted into intellectual property—on all this immense body of intellectual values the Glass Bead Game player plays like the organist on an organ.

Thus it is an esoteric game aiming at the very depth of the intellectual and creative life forces whose flow through the centuries is captured and unified at a focal point of lofty existence. In the final analysis, it is a game played by a chosen few with their past, the entire world and themselves.

Into this complex allegory extolling a myth of the most sublime humanism Hesse placed a central figure to give 'the inner reality of Castalia' a heightened credibility. The novel's subtitle reads: 'A tentative sketch of the life of Magister Ludi Joseph Knecht.' Knecht (which means servant in German, but relates etymologically to knight) is one of those gifted men, destined to move upwards until he reaches the highest position that Castalia has to offer, the office of the magister ludi, master of the glass bead game.

The ending is of Goethean proportions. Hesse realised that it is not enough to hear music and to visualise wise men of the past and future, 'poets and scholars and artists harmoniously building the hundred-gated cathedral of Mind'. From the liberating ironic laughter of the immortals in *The Steppenwolf* to the concept of servitude and love in his later writings, Hesse's affirmation attributed to Joseph Knecht made him find an ending to *The Glass Bead Game* determined by social consciousness.

As Goethe's Faust finally realises that 'only that which is fruitful is true' and that 'if you want to reach the infinite, traverse the finite to all sides', Hesse's Joseph Knecht too sees the limitations of Castalian universality which lacks the daily contact with the active and ever-changing life in the outside world. Knecht, who is eager to grow by sharing the miseries of the world, leaves Castalia to carry its wisdom into the world in the hope of adapting the acquired wisdom to its needs.

Knecht's tragic ending in sacrificing his life in a test of strength and, essentially, not to disappoint his pupil Tito, had meaning beyond the obvious for Hesse. Knecht's death is only logical if we are aware of Hesse's strong belief in the importance of the individual. In erasing his life, Knecht challenged the future of this boy. Tito, feeling responsible for the master's death, would be a changed man, Hesse believed. This sacrificial death 'would demand much greater things of [Tito] than he had ever before demanded of himself'. Hesse was convinced that only by influencing the individual can the world be bettered. This is why he could write to one of his young readers puzzled by this ending that the death of this superior man would be an 'admonishment and guidance forever and would educate [Tito] better than all sermons of wise men'.

POSTSCRIPT TO HIS LIFE

Hermann Hesse's popularity may wane with the change of literary fashion. But incontestable will remain the fact of his uniqueness as a human being, puzzled by his own complexities which he could not help analysing, and as a writer who could not help but put these puzzling parts together again.

With *The Glass Bead Game*, he must have felt that he summarised all he had to say. What followed after were recollections, autobiographic sketches, fairy tales, a few essays, and his *Rundbriefe*, letters he sent around to his friends all over the world. They are pieces of masterly prose. Most of them were collected under the title *Late Prose*, in which landscape descriptions of particular power, the pondering over past events, and memories of his childhood experiences take a prominent place.

We may visualise Hermann Hesse in his seventies and eighties as a man who could achieve what seemed to him the highest and noblest goal in mastering the glass bead game : to be full of autumnal gaiety. In spite of some physical suffering, he had a great deal of 'the gaiety of music which is nothing else but bravery', as he had described it in his last novel, 'as a serene, smiling striding and dancing through the horrors and inferno of the world'.

His eyesight weakened constantly. He had to learn to husband his energies, but he never stopped writing, painting, and taking walks. He rarely left his home in

Montagnola, and yet they were not lonely years. He hardly knew how to keep away the many visitors from his garden gate. Only the ageing Voltaire may have maintained a more voluminous and widespread correspondence than Hesse.

In 1960 he began to suffer from leukemia. He recovered, but during the many months that followed he was waiting for death. Eight days before he died at the age of eighty-five he wrote a poem. A few days later he wrote a second version of it and the day before his death, on the eighth of August 1962, a third version of one and the same poem which he called *The Creaking of a Broken Branch*. In it, he compared the broken branch to a dying man who is too tired of living as much as of the long process of dying. He still had the strength to produce a watercolour of the broken branch. The day before he died he picked up a few dead branches on his last walk through the woods. He loved to gather these branches for his daily bonfire in the garden. He stood in front of a tree, tore at a sick branch, but then he said: 'It still has some life in it'. Next morning Hermann Hesse was dead.

PART TWO

A FIGHTER IN SEARCH OF THE
ETERNAL TRUTHS

How deeply was Hesse involved in the events of his time? Are his critics justified in reproaching him for not having taken a more vociferous and active part in the political happenings of his time?

Hesse has too often been pictured as a romantic dreamer who rejected the realities of life. This stigma may have been inadvertently blown up to an heraldic sign for H.H. when the Anglo-Saxon young, in its desperate denial of the man-made madness of the time and in its rebellion against the past, elevated him to one of their gods or gurus. Although there was a great deal of the ascetic monk in him who bore a monastery with him wherever he went, he never left the actual world. He said of Turu, the Rainmaker, in *The Glass Bead Game* that he 'had little use for words, nor did he particularly like to hear other people talk'. This remark certainly referred to the monk in Hesse. But then he wanted to emphasise that he was not as *weltfremd* as people thought:

> Many people regarded him as eccentric, others as sullen, but he was neither. He knew much more about what went on around him than people would have given him credit for despite his learned and hermit-like absentmindedness.

Wherever possible Hesse made it quite clear that one should not mistake his predilection for withdrawal as a sign of an aversion towards reality. Facing the facts which the world forces upon us—even though we may protest at them—becomes a part of Hesse's visualisation of the total man. Whenever he saw wrong done, he could become a fighter for a just cause. I do not wish to sound like an apologist, but from a purely psychological viewpoint we cannot expect this nonconformist, who admittedly was happiest working in his garden or cell, to rush to the barricades. Nor was he a born orator. His faith in himself was as a writer, and his task, as he saw it, was to reach his readers with his ideas and counsel.

It has always been characteristic of Hesse that he did not believe in trying to change forms of government and political methods, but, as he stressed, 'we must begin with the shaping of the human personality if we want to have minds and men again who warrant a future'. Or, in a letter, written in 1951, he explained:

> I have never withdrawn from the problems of my time in the course of my development and have never lived in an ivory tower, as my political critics maintain—however, the first and most burning of my problems has never been the state, society, or the Church, but the single human being, the personality, the unique, not yet standardised, individual.

Or in a more puckish mood he once declared, varying the same theme: 'The difference between Marx and myself, except for the much greater dimensions of Marx, is this: Marx wants to change the world, but I the single human being. He turns to the masses, I to the individual.'

Time and again Hesse pointed at the roots of some of the evils which have beset mankind. There was nothing more hateful and stupid to him than boundaries separating one country from another. As long as peace and reason prevail no one takes them seriously; they only become sacred in days of friction and war. Thus he exlaimed : 'No fatherland and no ideals exist for me any longer, they are mere emblems for those gentlemen preparing the next battle.'

He saw the greatest danger for twentieth-century man in his escape from personal tasks and individual responsibilities into a 'religious overestimation' of the collective. He called this trend 'the worst enemy and corruptor of man'. Hesse felt that he who wishes to enjoy the protection of the herd knows nothing of the joy and beauty of his own mind and fantasy.

In his opinion two major phenomena are the curse of our time : the megalomania of technology and nationalism.

> It is they that give the present-day world its face and the image of itself. They have been responsible for two world wars and their consequences and before their fury is spent they will have further similar consequences.

Hesse considered it the most important task of our time to resist these two curses. 'To this resistance I have devoted my life, a ripple in the stream.'

It may come as a surprise that, in one of his letters, he advised his son Heiner on the benefits of socialism and that he often referred to Communism as a justified attempt of mankind to solve some basic questions of life. But he also stressed that the dictatorship of the proletariat denies the basic tenets of Communism and he pleaded for a just distribution of power and possessions between the workers and the bourgeois as the only solution for the future.

The existence of brutality and envy, maliciousness and extreme hatred must be taken for granted, since the majority of mankind is still in a subhuman state, with many beasts among them. We are surrounded by the meanness of man as much as we are threatened by death. Mankind has never been better or worse, and the future will not alter this condition if man cannot change and alter for the better his impatience, egotism, lack of love and tolerance. The best intention to change the world is useless without the salvation of the hidden self. Wherever Hesse spoke about war and peace, the ordeals and the tribulations of our time, the inward way was to him the only path leading to the inner and outer freedom of man.

When World War I was in its first year and the famous French pacifist Romain Rolland came to Switzerland in order to write, fight and work for a 'sacred union of the European spirit' (union sacrée de l'esprit européen), Hesse joined him in the struggle for peace and unity. From the very beginning of the war when Hesse lived in Berne to help care for imprisoned soldiers, he was already convinced of the necessity for such a union of the European spirit. In August 1915 these two pacifists met and decided to fight a war-mad world together, even though they had little chance of immediately realising their dream.

Ever since Hesse suffered from the realisation that senseless hatred dominates the world, he became so sensitive about it that he even rebuked his friend Rolland in a letter dated 15 January 1932, for using the expression 'Huns' with regard to the Germans in one of Rolland's essays on the war:

The expression 'Huns' is not worthy of you, my revered friend, and it would fit just as well a few excesses committed by your own countrymen. Men are beasts if no star watches over them, but we must not reproach a single people for having a monopoly of beastliness.

Soon after the war Hesse searched in himself for what made him so unhappy about the world. His 'being concerned', he felt, must have had something to do with his own guilt feelings, with his own inner disorder. And he asked himself:

In what way have I become an accomplice? And how can I become innocent again? For one can become innocent again at any time when one recognizes one's misery and guilt and bears the suffering instead of trying to blame someone else.

With prophetic insight he wrote to Romain Rolland in 1922 : 'There is something anarchic about the mood in Germany now, and also something religiously fanatic, it is a mood of world destruction as if the Reich of a thousand years were upon us.' In 1933 when Hitler seized power the Nazis arrogantly proclaimed the commencement of the thousand-year Reich. At about that time many young people, caught in the snares of Nazism, either condemned and berated Hesse for betraying their cause—he received innumerable letters vilifying him during the thirties—or asked for advice and help. 'For many years', Hesse said in one of his letters, 'half of my work has consisted of reading and replying to letters I receive from Germany, most of them from young people who come to me in their need, their hopes, ideals and despair.' He was always a conscientious letter-writer, but in those years he became compulsive about it as if a pressing need had forced him to reach those who could no longer find his writings in bookshops and libraries in Germany.

He had declared his enmity with Fascism and protested against the 'brutal, bloodthirsty stupidity of the people'. His books were, strangely enough, not publicly burnt by the Nazis, but Hesse was branded as a traitor. His works disappeared from the shelves, and soon afterwards there was no longer any paper to be had in Germany to print his books. He loathed the massive cruelties unleashed by Hitler and, as a German writer, he was sickened by the desecration of his language as a concomitant part of the dethronement of truth. Hesse has always loathed the hypocrisy and sham sentimentality which so often ridiculed the German spirit as he perceived it. Convinced of how the corruption of language reflects a corruption of feeling and thought (a Karl Krausian concept), he wrote in his essay, *Self-will*, in 1919:

> Just as reporters abuse the language when they term some senseless accident 'tragic' (which for those clowns is synonymous with 'deplorable'), is is an abuse of language to say—as is now fashionable, especially among stay-at-homes—that our poor soldiers, slaughtered at the front, died a 'heroic death'. That is sentimentality. Of course the soldiers who died in the war are worthy of our deepest sympathy . . . But that does not make them 'heroes'. The common soldier, at whom an officer bellows as he would at a dog, is not suddenly transformed into a hero by the bullet that kills him. To suppose that there can be millions of 'heroes' is in itself an absurdity.

Hesse cared little whether the world knew where he stood in this great historic struggle for man's survival. He was not concerned about his image, but much more about what he could contribute positively, what his words could mean to a single disturbed, uneasy mind. And he told himself: 'I can help a little all those who, like myself, sabotage the piggish, power-hungry politicians in their actions and thinking and who form islands of humaneness in the midst of devilry and murder.' Thus he wrote and spoke to those who turned to him in their quandary. He told them to believe in the spirit of man, not in the spirit of cannons : not to listen to so-called leaders, but to form their own opinion and then to have the courage of their own convictions. 'Those who think that our existence is tragic, but also sacred, have no right to shun their responsibility.'

Hesse never surrendered his belief in man 'as a wonderful potential which even in the deepest mire does not perish and which permits him to re-emerge from the depths of dehumanisation,' as he wrote in 1938, 'and I think this potential is so strong and so tempting that, time and again, it makes itself felt as hope and challenge.' Whatever fault one may find with his preference to live like a recluse and to send his 'belligerent' advisory and admonishing espistles from there to those who reached him in his hideout, he stood stubbornly by his principles, never wavering, never deviating from the only path he saw leading from man to man. He remained deaf to the din of the world, untouched by the vanity of vanities. When in 1954 a Chinese writer asked for permission to translate his books, Hesse replied : 'Today's China has forbidden Confucius and Lao Tse, or at least stigmatised them as undesirable, and in a country that at this moment of its history cannot bear its own classics I would not like to see any of my books translated.'

Hesse thought little of categorising man, but he realised that oneness must be sought and found behind and beyond all the contrasts. Recognising the complexities in man, he at least expected that people tried to unify their contrasting forces. He found neither the active nor the contemplative type to be exemplary. The man he looked for as an ideal personality was the one

65

who could be both alone with himself and a part of his community, capable of deeds and deep reflection. When weighing both contrasts on his own scales, the latter was no doubt the heavier. In his own defence he claimed that he presumably gave the contemplative more space in his writings than the active because he saw 'our world and time abound with active, efficient, agile people, unable to surrender to contemplation'.

Owing to his stress on the inward side of man, to his pacifist attitude and Eastern-oriented thinking, his political stance and involvement in the events of his time has, more often than not, been doubted and belittled. In the foreword to his book, *Krieg und Frieden* (translated as *If the War Goes on . . .*) he grappled with this question. He had come to politics very late, 'when I was almost forty, jolted awake by the gruesome reality of the war and profoundly horrified at the ease with which my colleagues and friends had enlisted in the service of Moloch'. He admitted that he wrote articles related to contemporary or political events only sporadically. But in his innumerable letters as much as in his works—from *The Steppenwolf* ('which was in part a cry of anguished warning against the approaching war') down to *The Glass Bead Game* which, despite its remoteness from current realities, deals with burning issues of man—he never closed his eyes to man's deepest concerns.

Thomas Mann and other writers changed their political mantle from nationalistic tendencies in their youth to the embrace of Communism in their old age. Hesse was convinced that it needed the greatest courage to remain true to oneself and not to yield easily to the pressures of politics and the mood of the time. He never wavered in his judgment nor did he believe in organised

protests or in joining a party of opposition since, as a
pacifist, he feared that militant resistance must of
necessity lead to violence and brutality :

> I wish to make it absolutely clear that I reject, and do not
> support, any attempt to change the world by force, also the
> socialist attempt, also other seemingly right and desirable
> attempts. It is always the wrong ones who are killed; and
> even if the right ones are, I cannot believe in the improving
> function of killing.

How unpolitical a person was he? Once his pen
slipped, and the unpolitical man blurted out that
'politics is not a matter of concern for me, otherwise I
would have long been a revolutionary'. At a moment
when his superego was neglectful of its duties, he
admitted where he would stand if the 'ifs' of his
philosophy of life had not opened other channels for
him.

When his logic and calmness prevail he is of course
against any revolution. In his essay, *Self-will*, written
under the impact of the First World War and the revolutions that followed it, he explained that 'revolution is
war; like all other war, it is a "prolongation of politics
by other means" '. In fashioning one's self-will he saw
a way of finding oneself, of being able 'to live out [one's]
destiny in freedom and purity'. This in itself is revolutionary since man places himself outside the established
lines of behaviourism and must then follow 'his own
law and will'. But he believed that in this case much
less of the evil existing in a well-ordered world would
occur, because man would stand beyond such temptations as money and power, and he would have questioned
and put aside such false virtues as patriotism and
obedience. Self-will is, in Hesse's eyes, also obedience,
but not to man-made laws; it is an obedience putting

67

greater demands on man, obedience to 'the one law I hold absolutely sacred—the law in himself, his own will . . . his only living destiny is the silent, ungainsayable law in his own heart to obey but which to the self-willed man is destiny and godhead'.

If we let every man act as his conscience dictates, we must be careful that if 'in the process he loses himself, his own soul', for then 'whatever he does will be worthless'. However contradictory some of Hesse's pronouncements may sound, all his thoughts return to his belief in man. Time and again he stresses that any change of political methods and forms of government leads inevitably to the eternal merry-go-round of renewed changes of political methods and forms of government. Again, it is only the shaping of the individual which can lead to any feasible salvation of mankind. Even though we know him to be right, it is obvious that this dictum belongs to the realm of utopia, and remains a dreamer's notion of how to improve a world lost to man, or how to correct man, victim of his world.

Essentially, Hesse was concerned only with man and not with mankind. What he said at the end of his long letter to a young German in 1919, who had turned to Hesse in his despair, not knowing what to believe and hope, had always been Hesse's deepest conviction : 'Our task as man is this : in our own unique personal lives, to take a short step on the road from animal to man.'

THE ESSAYIST

I am trying to stress in this short monograph how essential Hesse's instrinsic poetic awareness is to his prose as a novelist. There can be no doubt about the power of his poetic imagery, about the flow of his thoughts expressed in singing cadences, about his visualisations emerging from an androgynous state of part dream, part reality. An equally strong case could be made for Hesse's essayistic predilection.

The essayist in Hesse hid behind an autobiographical mirror and a narrative mask. His novels are shot through with essayistic forays and annotations. Moreover, the bulk of his writings is essayistic in nature : *Betrachtungen, Kurgast, Nürnberger Reise, Tractat vom Steppenwolf, Sinclairs Notizbuch, Wanderung, Gedenkblätter, Bilderbuch, Briefe,* and *Rundbriefe.* Most of his letters—and they fill volumes—were not idle communications but written with the full awareness of a literary statement of one kind or another.

The will to truth (which is never the only truth, as Hesse knew only too well) is one of the propelling forces of the essayist whose reflecting mind can attack any minor subject and turn it into a major one by adding his own thoughts. In the final analysis, the essay mirrors, in Montaigne's famous words, the writer : 'It is my self I portray.' It has always been a very literary mind with an imaginative urge to analyse and interpret that took to writing in essay form, a mind in love with the word, with great knowledgeability forced into a wide frame of reference, with the readiness of the only right word at the tip of his pen. All these pre-requisites can be found in Hesse and, moreover, the reluctant spirit of the missionary who wants to convince and help.

Hesse was an avid reader. As a young man his room was always littered with books, and deep into the night he would read, mostly by candlelight, to satisfy his demanding, hungry mind. His sons assured me that Hesse's serious eye troubles, his short-sightedness and headaches, which tortured him through many decades, were caused by his reckless reading habits in those early days in his life. In his long essay, *A Library of World Literature*, he gave us an inkling of the way he took, of the many varied journeys through the written and printed word, from his wondrous experience in his grandfather's library to his own discoveries of the literary treasures of the world, plunging into many minds, criss-crossing countries and cultures. He opened his essay, *Magic of the Book*, with the statement: 'Of the many worlds man did not receive as a gift from nature but had to create from his own mind, the greatest is the world of books.' He never stopped reading or being read to when his eyesight worsened. But he never read as the literary-minded aesthete who finds in well-hewn words a substitute for the reality of life. Books were experiences and explorations into the world of another life. Hesse once said, 'Books have value only when they lead to life, serve and are useful to one's existence. Every hour spent with a book is wasted if not a spark of strength, a feeling of rejuvenation, a touch of newness result from it.'

Hesse's style moved from the simplistic and romantically evocative to the meditative and poetically lofty; it always had a touch of restrained passion and a passionately expressed philosophy. He was a man of many nuances and different roots. For him, language had a mysterious quality because, inherently, every sentence has a melody of its own which sings in us and which the writer liberates and gives a harmonic texture with counterpoints of interplay and contrasts. But words also have a colour scale, tinges and shades in their visual tonality. It is in keeping with Hesse's philosophy of life that he believed in the language as being good and right when it is the expression of a strong and genuine experience. The writer is not necessarily master of his own words. 'When he puts down a word with which he intended to express something subjectively limited, a warning, a stream of acoustic, optic, and emotional associations' take command and may guide him unexpected ways. Hesse saw something mystic and magic, rhythmic and colourful emerging from language, from its primal wells of which the writer is unaware, but which supports him as much as it may distract him. This proved to Hesse that language is not only an expressive tool, 'but a creative power, less sensible but more potent than the poet'.

These feelings about the writer's relationship to his language kept Hesse from becoming a pioneer in new forms and expressions in an age of experimentation. He was too responsible a craftsman, too conscious of his mission as an artist to give in to experimentation for the sake of experimenting. What he constantly experimented with was his thinking, his endeavour to penetrate the mystery of life, man's many-faceted complexities. As a matter of fact, he prided himself on being a man of the past, a traditionalist. 'I never strived for the new in form, for being an avant-gardist and pacemaker,' he admitted.

With a surprising and mostly deceptive simplicity as the hallmark of his style, with a melody all its own, he developed a strong feeling for form and clarity. Despite his contemplative attitude, a seemingly ineradicable part of his nature, his essays move along swiftly and lucidly. An essayist is at his best when his style does not indulge in a descriptive, leisurely pace, but drives on to its point with relentless pithiness. The essays carrying the H.H. imprint are of a different kind. The aphorism—and in certain polemical circumstances the epigram—would, in nuce, reflect the essayistic talent. But even at his most polemical in his essays, Hesse never played the role of the aggressive controversialist. Where others shoot off their poisonous arrows with epigrammatic fury, he opened his heart, pleading for his cause. It is never the bravura sentence, the virtuosity of a skilfully expressed thought with which he dazzles, but it is the credibilty of his belief with which he convinces. One can feel that the conveyed dictum is the result of his own experience. Even an expressed truism rings true and wise because it still shows something of the wounds and conflicts which made him write it. Some of the strong impulses for the essayist in Hesse were his own inner contradictions for which he tried to find a common temperamental denominator.

To distil the essence of the polarity of his problems was not easy for Hesse. But there was a compulsive need in him to come to terms with himself and through himself with the world. This may also explain his need to communicate through letters and may have made him one of the most prolific letter writers in the age of the telephone. His letters take a very special place within his oeuvre. They are a repository of daily asides; of exhortative and explanatory replies to desperate pleas and outcries; and answers to inconsequential questions which stimulated Hesse to plunge into a discussion with himself. Perhaps quite unconsciously, his anachronistic stance and antagonistic attitude towards this mechanised era made him return to an earlier century in which fiction and essay were written in the form of letters. Moreover, Hesse became the letter-writing victim of his own conviction which made him equate the poet with priesthood. It was an archetypically missionary gesture to reach out to those in apparent need of help. Sometimes his words had overtones of the preacher.

Besides the therapeutic effect in answering many of the thousands of letters he received year after year, it is fascinating to consider that so many people should have turned to a man whose work was so self-reflective and aloof from actualities and realities. It seems that, recognising his fictionalised personality in his personalised fiction, the readers thought they knew the writer personally and well enough to have the right to address him. Hesse realised this when he said :

> I do not think that it is the literary quality of my books which attracts the majority of my readers. I rather think that most of them recognise or sense in my work and my person the representative of a psychological type to which they belong . . . they find their own mentality, their own psychic make-up and problems expressed and confirmed.

He and his wife, Ninon, preserved letters occasionally 'whose theme seemed characteristic to us,' he wrote in a note closing the second edition of *Letters*, 'or in which we found a problem of general interest particularly well expressed'. These letters take the place of a platform from which he addressed the world through the addressee. He teaches without letting us feel that he teaches. For example, in writing to Miss G. D.stud phil. in Freiburg i.B., in 1930, he addressed German youth :

> You are full of ambitions, you have many desires, you have many dark drives which somehow would like to be sublimated. What you don't have is *awe*. It's not your fault. But without awe all spirit is an evil spirit... *The Steppenwolf* not only deals with jazz music and girls, but also with Mozart and the immortals. And thus my entire life stood under the sign of an attempt to commitment and devotion, to religion ... Even if I must despair of my time and myself, nevertheless, awe for life and the possibility of its meaningfulness cannot be cast out, and if I would have to stand alone, if I were to make myself ridiculous—I would hold on to it ... simply because I do not want to live without awe, without devotion to a god.

Hesse feels challenged by some of the people who write to him and, as he did in his fictional accounts of himself, he invites them in his replies to follow him on his journeys through the labyrinth of his own experiences while acting as an erudite guide and an entertaining host. But he does not want them to follow him blindly, to see in him a 'leader'. As early as 1932 when German youth desperately looked for someone who would 'lead' them, Hesse rejected the idea of playing this role. In the answer to an open letter in which the mission of a great writer was equated with his duty to lead, Hesse replied :

> You maintain that a writer who has gained the trust of many readers cannot avoid accepting the duty of leadership. I admit that I have come to hate the word 'leader', a so often misused word by the young people in Germany today.
>
> Only he who does not want to accept responsibility and does not want to think for himself needs and asks for a leader. The poet—as much as his existence is still possible in our time and culture—cannot accept such a task. True, he should show responsibility, he should be like a model for others, but ... he

should have the decency to renounce leadership and 'wisdom' and be strong enough not to have forced upon him the role of the one who knows or of the priest, since he himself is only one who surmises and suffers. That so many and mainly young people find something in my works which makes them trust me, has a simple explanation: there are many who suffer as I do, who seek meaning and faith, who despair of their time and yet sense and admire the divine behind this and any other time ... I do not wish to give or promise more than I have. I am a sufferer in the turmoil of our age, not someone who can lead others to escape it. I am willing to walk through it as if it were hell itself in the hope of finding beyond it a new innocence and a more dignified life, but I am unable to pretend that we have already arrived there.

This is why I do not think that my life is without meaning, that I have no mission whatsoever. To persevere in the midst of chaos, to be able to wait, to feel humility for life even there where its apparent senselessness is frightening—these are also virtues, particularly in days when new pronunciations of world-historic happenings, when new interpretations of life, new programmes of all kinds come so cheap.

Only one who can be nobler than a king can refuse the burden of a crown and only a sage who knows how he himself gropes for the key to wisdom can be as simple as Hesse was. Is this reply to a letter written in 1932 still valid in our own time so many years later? Life in the nuclear and electronic age may have changed, its perils and possibilities have become magnified, but the doubts, hopes and needs of the young have not changed. This is why Hermann Hesse's voice has become meaningful again for a new generation in despair. Reading through his now collected letters we hear the voice of someone who suffered and found words of comfort for our own suffering. His voice still tells us that we must overcome 'the sickness of the times themselves' as it is reflected within us and that we can do it by walking step by step through frustration to fulfillment and by growing into new dimensions of our awareness.

His *Rundbriefe* were written between 1947 and 1954 when Hesse was in his seventies. I can only describe these essayistic musings of an old man waiting for death with the German word 'Wehmut' whose transliteration would be sweet melancholy or sadness. But beyond this sombre and mournful mood, Hesse's *Rundbriefe*, a string of long farewell epistles, reveal the strength of an 'old and wise' man—as he was so often addressed in those years—who takes issue with life.

There is an undertone in these letters as if they were written from across a bridge ('life thus becomes a kind of playful sur-reality'), as if they exuded a strange feeling of no longer being here, of almost longing for death. In his *Aprilbrief*, 1952, he wrote :

> We assume that in our young years we have also experienced most intensely and glowingly the sight of a flowering tree, a cloud formation, a storm, and yet for the very experience I mean old age is needed, an endless sum of events, experiences, thoughts, feelings, suffering, a certain thinning of our vital drives are needed, a certain frailty and proximity of death—and all this to perceive God, spirit, and secret in a little revelation of nature, the collapse of contrasts, the great oneness. The young ones can certainly experience the same, but rarer and without such oneness of feelings and thoughts, of sensuous and spiritual experience, of attraction and awareness.

Although these *Rundbriefe* were usually addressed to 'My Dear Friends' and were sent to Hesse's many friends all over the world, I cannot help feeling that they were not addressed to anyone except himself as literary essays on remembrances of things past.

Most of Hesse's letters are miniature essays telescoping

the problems of a whole era in a few paragraphs, on occasion ending with an epigrammatic fury rare in Hesse. Such a letter was directed to Professor J. W. Hauer, Tübingen, in May 1935, in which on two printed pages the entire problem of morality and Christianity ('Thou shalt not kill') as juxtaposed to the brutality of Nazism is unfolded. The letter ends with a prediction of the coming holocaust: 'Enough for today. I only tried to indicate a few thoughts. It is like at the time of the Reformation: One thinks one philosophises and merely prepares a Thirty Years War.'

The range of his letters is amazing. There is one of the finest love letters written from Zürich in April 1928 to his wife Ninon who happened to be in Paris at the time. The irony of loneliness details the little events of his daily life and closes: 'Running around in the city so alone, without eyes—for you have taken them with you—is actually terribly boring . . . if it rains and no bird sings and you being so far away, then life is not really up to much.'

At the opposite end we find letters addressed to well-known personalities. I single out a letter written to André Gide in January 1951, a time in which Hesse felt he was living 'in a state of resigned tiredness':

The people of our kind, so it seems, have become rare and begin to feel lonesome, therefore it is with happiness and consolation that I know you as a lover and defender of freedom, of personality, self-will, and individual responsibility. The majority of our younger colleagues and, unfortunately, so many of our own generation strive for quite different things, for *Gleichschaltung* to the point of self-destruction. With each deviation of a former comrade to churches and collectives, with each desertion of a colleague who became too tired or desperate to be able to remain a self-responsible loner, the world becomes poorer for us and to go on living harder. I

77

suppose you feel the same. Once more accept the greeting of an old individualist who does not think of joining one of the great machineries.

It cannot be easily refuted that the recluse H.H., living in the imaginary Castalia of the Ticino, needed to keep in touch with the world and people to whom he wanted to be of service—even though from a distance. But his readiness to serve—a thought so strongly expressed in *The Journey to the East*—and to listen to the problems of his letter-writers with great attention, built an imaginary bridge from his *sanctum sanctorum* into the regions of ordinary human existence.

The end of World War I and the collapse of all the old values coincided with the completion of Hesse's inner change, with the realisation that

> I found war and all murderous instincts of the world, all its wantonness, its crude thirst for pleasure, all its cowardice reflected in myself; I had first to lose my self-respect, then the contempt for myself; I had nothing else to do but to extend a glimpse into the chaos to its very end with the often flaring-up and dying-out hope to find nature and innocence again beyond the chaos.

It was a grave period not only in the world at large, but also in the private world of H.H. who, in the spring of 1919, withdrew 'into a remote corner of Switzerland to become a hermit'. He questioned his guilt as a part of mankind's guilt and asked himself how he could become innocent again. He gave himself the following answer: 'One can always become innocent again if, recognising one's suffering and guilt, one accepts them and follows them through to their very end instead of seeking the guilt with others.' He gave the chaos around him a deeper, penetrating look. The immediate results were the novels *Demian* and *Klein and Wagner* as well as a few essays published under the title: *Glimpse Into Chaos*.

The most impressive essay in this volume is 'The Brothers Karamazov or The Decline of Europe'. He subtitled it 'Thoughts on Reading Dostoevsky' and tried to discredit himself as an essayist by saying that he could not bring his thoughts into a cohesive and pleasing form since he lacked the talent for it and that he did not wish to be presumptuous like other authors who try to impress the reader with a few notions they present as an essay. With this apologetic statement his brilliant essay begins.

Hesse's concept of the polarities is found here again in the Russian man who worships a God who is Satan as well. The ideal of the Karamazovs, 'an age-old, Asiatic-occult ideal' begins to spread over Europe and devour it, their 'departure from all established ethics and morality in favour of an attempt to understand everything, to accept everything, of a new, dangerous, gruesome sanctity, as prognosticated by the old man Sosima . . .' This downfall from inner grace must, in Hesse's eyes, be visualised as 'a return to the mother, to all sources, the Faustian "mothers" and will, as a matter of course, lead to a rebirth as all death does on earth'. This is a return to the dark world of unconsciousness in which the contrasts and their evaluations become eliminated, in which the criminal will exists side by side with the poetic and saintly in man as in Karamazov who is 'murderer and judge at once, a ruffian and the gentlest soul, he is the most perfect egotist as much as a hero capable of the most perfect sacrifice'. The destruction of Europe will come with chaos and amorality, with

79

revolutions of great brutality followed by crime, corruption, murder and vice.

Written at the end of a holocaust which we conveniently summed up with the Roman number I, Hesse realised that chaos would beget chaos, with more cataclysmic developments to come. True enough, Chaos II and an existential world, resigned to the gesture of futility, with demonic laughter about its own absurdity came next. With prophetic vision Hesse saw beyond these stages that corruption and vice would dance to the drumbeats of brutality.

Dostoevsky's *Idiot*, Prince Myshkin, however, may point the way to a decisive revaluation of the chaos within. In his total isolation from his environment, he sees reality in a different light from everyone else, still clinging to defunct orders and morals. 'He who feels spirit and nature, good and evil as interchangeable, and if only for a moment, is the most formidable enemy of any order. For there the contrary of order begins, there chaos starts'. Prince Myshkin is a magic individual who believes in the reversion of all statutes, 'he does not smash tablets of laws, he only turns them around to show that the contrary is engraved on the reverse side'.

What Hesse found so frightening about Dostoevsky's novel is not that sick bodies and minds gesture like saints and act like criminals, but that the European youth, and particularly the Germans among them, accepted these fictional figures because they discovered similar features in their own soul. Hesse thought that we cannot help going through Myshkin. Hesse demanded 'magic thinking', the acceptance of chaos. 'Return to disorder, return to the unconscious, the shapeless, the animal, and still further back beyond the animal to all beginning.' But Hesse did not visualise this as the ultimate objective. This would be a new point of departure to reorientate ourselves, 'to find forgotten drives and chances for development at the roots of our being'. No proclamations, programmes and revolutions will help us find ourselves again. Hesse suggested that everyone of us will, from time to time and at one point or another, have to stand 'at the Myshkinian border where the truths stop and new ones can begin'.

I wonder why so relatively little has ever been made of Hesse the essayist. True, an Anglo-Saxon writer, an American who became anglicised, T. S. Eliot, read *Glimpse Into Chaos* when it was first published. He was so impressed that he referred to it in his *Notes on 'The Waste Land'*, quoting from it in German:

> Half of Europe by now, at least half of Eastern Europe is already on the way to chaos, it drives drunken in holy madness along the precipice while singing as Dmitri Karamazov sang, drunken and hymning. The burgher laughs about these songs as if he were insulted, the saint and seer hears them with tears in his eyes.

T. S. Eliot, like Hesse, was a poet turned essayist. He recognised Hesse's greatness, not as a lyricist, because as a writer of verses Eliot was light-years ahead of Hesse, but as the essayist who in *Glimpse Into Chaos* expressed Eliot's thoughts that went into *The Waste Land*: despair and disgust, disenchantment and disillusionment. In a conversational virtuoso style Eliot caught the post-war period in its fears and lusts, in its hollowness waiting for a way out, a sign of redemption. He echoed Hesse's feelings when he wrote the fifth section, entitled *What The Thunder Said*, when he heard 'murmur of maternal lamentation' and saw 'hooded hordes swarming over endless plains' and 'falling towers' of a lost civilisation: 'Jerusalem Athens Alexandria/Vienna London/Unreal.'

The Waste Land was published two years after *Glimpse Into Chaos*. In May of that year, 1922, Eliot journeyed to Montagnola to meet Hermann Hesse. By then, however, Hesse had come out of the tunnel of darkness that had frightened him. He had left the Myshkinian border, as he described it in 'Thoughts on Dostoevsky's Idiot', the old chaotic truths had stopped and beyond the borders Hesse had started from first principles to find himself again. When Eliot met him, Hesse was a happier man. His new truths were in print by then, in the poetic apotheosis of eternal unification : *Siddhartha*.

HESSE'S BRAND OF HUMOUR

> With Hesse the expression alone is restrained, not the feeling or the thought; and what tempers the expression of these things is the exquisite feeling of fitness, reserve and harmony, and, with relationship to cosmos, the interdependence of things; it is also a certain latent irony, of which few Germans seem to be capable, and whose total absence so often spoils so many works of so many authors who take themselves terribly seriously. Hesse's irony, so charming in quality, seems to me to depend on the faculty of leaving himself behind without complacency; it is a form of modesty that becomes all the more attractive because more gifts and virtues accompany it.

With these words André Gide tries to define some of the more significant qualities in Hesse's work. Irony is Hesse's brand of humour. Irony hides behind subtle understatements, it avoids being obvious and immediately recognisable. It often disguises itself as allegory because, masqueraded, it feels safe in presenting its vital ideas.

Gide's remark that Hesse had the ability to be objective is corroborated by Hesse's own statement in *The Steppenwolf* when Pablo prepares Harry for a fruitful attendance at his magic theatre. Pablo asks him to look into the mirror and observe the picture with sincere laughter in order to extinguish it : 'You are here in a school for humour, you are to learn to laugh. All true humour begins when a man ceases to take himself seriously.'

Hesse saw humour, in its highest function, as a handmaiden to his philosophy of life. He alluded to it when, again in *The Steppenwolf*, he said :

> To live in the world as if it were not the world, to respect the law and yet to stand above it, to possess as if possession did not exist, to resign yourself as if there had been nothing to be renounced—all these popular and often formulated demands of life's profound wisdom can only be realised by humour.

This postulate sounds very much as if Harry Haller and Hermann Hesse rolled in one had their fun translating Friedrich Schiller's pronouncement on the highest goal of comedy and humour into their own feelings. In his essay *On Naive and Sentimental Poetry* Schiller said :

> If tragedy proceeds from a more important premise, one must admit, on the other hand, that comedy moves towards a greater goal, and comedy would, if it reached this goal, make all tragedy superfluous and impossible. Its goal is identical with the highest towards which men can strive: to be free from passions, to always look about oneself with a clear and unperturbed mind, to be ever ready for accidents rather than fate and to laugh more about incongruencies than to be angry or weep about meanness.

It could be claimed with some justification that a humorous undercurrent ran through Hermann Hesse's rather low-keyed, pensive, slightly melancholy but highly self-willed and tenacious make-up. Next to the testimony of his family I cannot call a worthier friend of his to the witness stand than Thomas Mann, who wrote a congratulatory article on Hesse's sixtieth birthday in the *Neue Zürcher Zeitung*:

> ... I also love the man and the human being in him, the serenely contemplative, roguish-kind way, the deep beautiful look of his unfortunately sick eyes whose blue lights up the lean and sharply profiled face of an old Swabian peasant.

Mann's description of the contrasting qualities underlining the philosophic inclination and the boyish and mischievous temperament is indicative of Hesse's make-up. His wit was always embedded in a knowing kindness and his fury or bad temper found an outlet in irony.

His son Bruno remembered a scene which was characteristic for the tacit manner in which he handled impatience and anger. As a child, Bruno Hesse was together with his mother and father on an excursion. Child and mother wanted to ascend a mountain, but his father was disinclined to undertake the trip. Mother and son had hardly turned around when Hermann Hesse was, without any discussion, on the next train taking him home. Hesse's will knew of no impediment for his determined action, his anger and wit never combined forces for a bitter attack. He could take a stand, but he also understood only too well the many-sidedness of each question, the complexities of human nature, the tendency of fixed notions to become aggressive. Anger and wit hid behind the protective mantle of irony.

Another incident may illuminate his self-contained reactions. In July 1958, the German magazine, *Der Spiegel*, known, among other things, for its aggressiveness, published in its writers section a long essay, a negative appreciation of Hermann Hesse under the title: *Hermann Hesse in the Vegetable Garden*. This was four years before his death. His wife Ninon tried to keep this article out of his sight which, by then, was so poor that he depended on being read to most of the time. Every member of the family was instructed not to read this article to him, but inadvertently his son Bruno began to read it aloud, only to stop quickly when he realised that this was the article which should not have come to his father's attention. Strangely enough,

Hesse knew about it and consoled his despairing son: 'We must not hold it against them. That's their profession. They make a living on being vicious about most people they write about. I suppose it was my turn.'

Hesse's letters and essays contain many paragraphs in which he either mocked himself or the world. Many ironic asides give a special timbre to his writings. In a letter to Ninon in 1928 he reported on his daily activities in Zürich and, apologetically, reminded her of his essay in praise of idleness:

> If I were not basically a very diligent man, how could I have ever hit upon the idea of writing a paean and theories on idleness? The born, ingenious idlers have never been known to do anything like that.

One of the earlier essays, *Conversation With a Stove*, is a brief, whimsical *tour de force*, written in an ironic tone from beginning to the end. Hesse introduces himself to the stove Franklin which turns out to be from Italy with the name Francolino. Hesse is surprised that an Italian stove should have an American name: Isn't that strange? The reply:

> Strange? No, it is one of the secret laws, you know. A secret law of interrelations and supplementations, nature is full of such laws. Cowardly people have folk songs extolling courage. Loveless people have stage plays extolling love. The same happens with us stoves. An Italian stove mostly has an American name, in the way a German stove mostly has a Greek one. They are German, and believe me, they give no more heat than I do, but they are called Eureka or Phoenix or Hector's Farewell. This stirs great memories. That's why I am called Franklin. I am a stove and, based on certain characteristics, I could just as well be a statesman. I have a big mouth, consume much, spend little warmth, spit smoke

through a pipe, have a good name and arouse great
memories. That's how it is with me.

Hesse continues to interview the stove which finally
wants to put a determined end to this conversation :

> How much you ask! Is it known to you that man is the
> only being wanting to make some sense of things. For all of
> nature the oak is an oak, the wind a wind, the fire a fire. For
> man, however, everything is different, makes sense, is rele-
> vant! Everything becomes sacred, is a symbol. A homicide
> is the deed of a hero, an epidemic a sign of God, a war is
> evolution. Why do you expect a stove to be nothing but a
> stove? No, it too is a symbol, a monument, a prophet ... This
> is why a stove does not see its sole destiny in giving a bit of
> heat.

There is a touch of irony in Hesse's attempt to teach
himself a lesson in *The Steppenwolf* by depicting an
intellectual in despair, a man losing faith in life and the
ideals of the spirit. He learns to accept the joys of the
senses and the trivialities of existence, previously feared
and rejected, when he realises through the magic of
make-believe that his beloved immortals, Goethe and
Mozart, never rejected reality but sublimated and
transcended it. He learns all this by learning to laugh,
by imitating the laughter of the immortals.

There is laughter throughout this novel in minor and
major keys and for very different reasons, laughter as the
realisation that only humour can turn dissonances into
harmony and can make us recapture a sense of the
higher values of life. 'A refreshing laughter rose up in
me,' Harry Haller, the steppenwolf, realises at the outset
of his magic trip. After having danced with Hermine, he
'heard a laugh ring out, an extraordinarily clear and
merry peal of laughter ... It was a laugh, made of
crystal and ice, bright and radiant ...' The laugh of the

immortals is the key to his understanding. When Harry recalled his dream of Goethe 'when he laughed so in-humanly', he suddenly seemed to understand Goethe's laughter. 'It was a laughter without an object. It was simply light and lucidity. It was that which is left over when a true man has passed through all the sufferings ... and got through to eternity ...'

Pablo's eyes always laughed and Pablo laughed aloud as he spoke because it was also Mozart who laughed out of him. Mozart said to Harry: 'How pathetic you always are. But you will learn humour yet, Harry. Humour is always gallows-humour, and it is on the gallows you are now constrained to learn it.' Haller is found guilty of having confounded the imaginative, the magic of life, with reality. He is laughed out of court by 'a laughter in full chorus, a frightful laughter of the other world ...' At his journey's end, after having been told that he 'broke through the humour' of the Magic Theatre making a mess of it, he finally understood:

> I understand Mozart, and somewhere behind me I heard his ghastly laughter. I knew that all the hundred thousand pieces of life's game were in my pocket ... One day I would be a better hand at the game. One day I would learn how to laugh.

Longfellow called Jean Paul 'The Only-One,' and Johann Paul Friedrich Richter was a unique German Romantic, still imbued with rationalist elements from the Enlightenment, a strange cross between a satirist and sentimentalist, a writer whose prose was poetic in a colourful and profound way. Jean Paul was, no doubt, godfather to Hesse's visitor at the spa of Baden. In his introduction he reminds the reader of Jean Paul's wonderful *Dr. Katzenbergers Spa Journey*, among the many stories about spas 'a bird of paradise among the sparrows', but this thought did not keep him from letting his 'sparrow fly after this bird of paradise'.

Whether rheumatic pains can arouse a reaction of ironic humour and even sarcasm is a question for physiologists to decide. The facts are that occasionally humorous effects were achieved in earlier Hesse novels, but he became more conscious of his ironic gift and more skilful in its application during his stay in Baden for a cure of his sciatica. Hesse's first and most outstanding biographer, Hugo Ball, insinuates that Hesse's apparent pains were not quite justified by the medical findings. 'There was a considerable plus of sensibility. Some strange plus was added in his reactions to his doctors and environment.' There are indications of a neurosis, negated in a humorous manner. Hesse, the writer, looks at Hesse, the visitor to the spa, as a seemingly detached observer, and much of the ironic wit of the book lies in the struggle between the two Hesses. 'The stiffer our bones become,' he wrote, 'all the more urgently do we require an elastic, two-sided bipolar way of thinking.'

In the beginning Hesse is an ever-complaining guest, at odds more with himself than his environment. The two Hesses find one another while wrestling with the problem of existing side by side (or room by room) with a Dutchman first pictured with utter disgust but whom he learns to accept with love and humour as one should accept reality:

My task was quite clear: I had to do away with worthless hatred, I had to love the Dutchman. Let him spit and bellow; I was superior to him, I was safe. If I succeeded in loving him, then all his well-being, all his vitality could no longer help him. Then he would be mine, then his image could no

89

longer resist the idea of unity. Well then, the goal was worthwhile, I simply had to make good use of my sleepless nights.

With gentle ironic overtones Hesse tries to juxtapose
himself as a healthy specimen against a sick society until
he unmasks himself. As Hugo Ball indicates, these
symptoms became symbols and Hesse's whimsical report
of a querulous visitor to a spa can be looked at like a
mirror reflection of a sick society.

How very private Hesse's humour could be and how
triumphantly his irony could assume a roguish smile is
proved by his *Journey to the East*. Irony is at the core
and forms the colourful glaze of this story. Not only is
it an ironic title since the journey gets nowhere except
to the heart of Hesse's matter (or to the matter of his
heart), but it is also shot through with in-jokes, meaningful only to a few initiated readers. Many incidents were
inspired by certain experiences of the author, such as
the Chinese Temple which refers to a friend's home in
Winterthur. Most of the characters are more blatantly
introduced under recognisable synonyms (when he speaks
of 'Ninon, known as "the foreigner" '—the obvious
reference is to his wife Ninon whose maiden name was
Ausländer, meaning foreigner in German). He re-
introduces fictional characters from his own works :
Pablo and Lauscher taking part in a celebration; so are
characters of history, the composer Hugo Wolf, the
Romantic poet Brentano, and some of his closest
friends.

Every paragraph bristles with ironic tricks and
allusions of a very private nature—which, however, does
not impair the weightiness of the story's universal
validity. It is one of the stories in which we discover
Hesse in a playful, almost impish mood. Probably this
lightness of his poetic pen had, at that time, very much

to do with his personal happiness that followed his marriage with Ninon, the 'foreigner'. *Journey to the East* was the first major product of his third and final marriage. Can we assume that Hesse thought of marriage as a happy journey leading nowhere, 'a mêlée of life and poetry', and teaching us the great lesson of the highest ideal of life: to serve. Hesse must permit his interpreters to play the ironic game as much as he did.

On the surface his final work, *The Glass Bead Game*, is a *Bildungsroman* telling of the personal development of a certain Joseph Knecht. Thomas Mann was the first to recognise the hidden humour in the book and expressed his concern that this magnum opus will only be read with 'dead-earnest respect.' He feared that very few readers would be able to understand Hesse's private jokes with which he already enjoyed himself in *The Journey to the East*, introducing and characterising his friends through veiled names. He undoubtedly liked to play this game of onomastic clownery. For example, Thomas von der Trave is a portrait of Thomas Mann, Fritz Tegularius, 'that sublime acrobat of *The Glass Bead Game*', is the difficult and problematic figure of Friedrich Nietzsche, and Father Jacobus is no one else but the historian Jakob Burckhardt whom Hesse revered.

Thomas Mann recognised the characters à clef and the many references and quotations as 'a cunning artistic joke'. Hesse skilfully masked the humour with 'a grave scholarly attitude', so that its parodistic points can easily get lost. Thomas Mann's fears were fully justified. Hesse's subtlety of irony, particularly in a setting of literary parody, can only be spotted by a limited elite of literati. The enjoyment of the initiate and connoisseur may add another dimension to the book which, however, is in no way the poorer if it does not unlock Hesse's secret cabinet of merry mirrors to everyone.

Hesse was quite aware of what created in him a predilection for humour, and for his special kind of humour. In *The Nuremberg Journey* Hesse admits to belonging to those people who 'perceive life as a whole as suffering and pain, not only conceptually out of a literary-aesthetical pessimism, but physically and in real terms'. However, such people have an even greater need to overcompensate for their talent for perceiving pain. In their almost compulsive desire to embrace the gayer aspects of life, 'Nature accomplishes something highly beautiful and complicated in this way, something that almost all people respect : humour.' Hesse visualised that the thing one calls humour is 'a crystal which grows only in deep and lasting pain and, after all, belongs to the better products of mankind.' He also thought that, under the pressure of life, 'I retreat into humour . . . an attempt to bridge the gap between the ideal and experience.'

He remarks in *The Nuremberg Journal* that his little refined taste permits him to visit cinemas and that he numbers among the sincerest 'and, as I believe, the most understanding admirers of Chaplin'. A few pages later Hesse stresses with an almost melancholy gesture that we must laugh about the games life plays with us. In his journey he passed through Munich where he inquired whether he could find in this city a genuine and classic comedian, adding apologetically that he wished to see a fine comedian because to laugh seemed to him to be a good and very desirable thing. He saw the famous Valentin in his grotesque and tragic moments, grotesque in their tragedy and tragic in their grotesqueries. 'The greater the comedian is, the more frightful and helpless in reducing our stupidity and our stupid, anxious human lot to a comic formula, the more we must laugh!' Also, the humorists may write whatever they may, in reality they vary only one theme: 'The wondrous sadness and, I may be forgiven for the expression, the shittiness of human life and the amazement about the fact that this pitiful existence can nevertheless be beautiful and priceless.'

After having said all this, Hesse concludes his spiritual travelogue with the feeling that he had always somehow known that perhaps 'a humorist was hidden in me, but then, of course, I was quite well off. The humorist in me had not yet a chance to develop fully since I had not been sufficiently badly off.'

Spiritually, Hesse was badly off enough in that period of his life. For a great deal of ironic laughter, of sarcastic whiplashing of himself and the world can be heard and seen in *The Steppenwolf*, the book that followed. It was not a book 'of a man despairing, but a man believing', Hesse said of it in 1961. But in that year, a year before his death, he could easily see how the 'Steppenwolf's world of suffering' was juxtaposed by 'a positive, serene, superpersonal and timeless world of faith'.

However, he must have thought of it as a sharper attack on the ills of mankind when he wrote it in the mid-twenties with the spectre of another apocalyptic event in the making; and with *The Steppenwolf* making his readers aware of their own time and problems as well as self-critical of their 'whole present life whose hell you do not want your poet to show you', as he wrote in a letter. In 1961 Hesse could smile a resigned smile and, for all we know, he may already have laughed the laugh of the immortals.

MUSIC, NATURE AND PAINTING

In Hesse's *Hermann Lauscher* we read this confession:
'What else do I expect from each day but a certain
mood, a colour very much its own and, if I am lucky,
a song,' All people whose sensibilities are attuned to the
inexplicable wonders of the world and to the mysterious
darkness and depths of their own being, live with music
as a daily need and a means of escape. Hesse and music
are inseparable. His mother reported about him that
'he could sing little songs he had made up himself' and
that as a four-year-old he 'sings in bed often for a long,
long time extemporaneously quite nice things and
rhymes. . .'

At the age of nine he received a violin and later
learned to play the flute. Music opened a new world to
him, something quite aside from everything else, something deep within 'in which innumerable sensations,
joys and woes could gather'. He later said: 'With violin
and a little singing I made my first steps into music
when I was a boy.' In speaking of his parents, Hesse
identified his father with the love of poetry and the
visual arts, while music was a world related to his
mother. This is important in his case since music was
an ever-ready means of departure and refuge, a 'deep
consolation and justification for all life'. He said of his
hero in *Gertrud* that 'of all invisible powers music has
the strongest hold on him and is destined to rule him'.
Music is the one touch-stone in life for an understanding
between two people. In 1919, after his first marriage

had come to an end in which, if nothing else, music had tied two people together, he had Iris say in a fable :
'If I should live with a man, it must be one whose music is well and finely attuned to mine and whose only desire must be that his music sounds well and pure together with mine . . .'

To make of life a song and pure music was one of Hesse's goals. He was convinced that one cannot tear music out of one's heart without bleeding to death. But Hesse was also aware of the negative implications when the mind is totally immersed in music, namely, of awakening false illusions utterly detached from reality, as has often been the case with the romantic German genius. We cannot rule out that whenever Hesse felt he had to escape his inner dissonances and the outside din, music remained his 'last and most profound consolation'. Music, in its abstract and, at the same time, most subjective nature, seemed close to the poetic essence of his being, never so close as to distract him yet always close enough to inspire him.

In his *Preface of a Poet to his Selected Works* Hesse wrote in 1921 that 'lyric poetry is not merely making verses, it is, above all, making music'. On the other hand, prose must sing too, and most of Hesse's prose has a melodic warmth. Hesse goes a step further and refers to music in prose as an attempt at heightening the level of prose to an imaginatively unrhymed but rhythmically defined prose form as in Nietzsche's *Thus Spake Zarathustra*. The most outstanding example of the strong rhythmic pattern in Hesse's prose is *Siddhartha*, full of lovely cadences and rhythmic cascades. He spoke of *The Steppenwolf* as a book 'built around the intermezzo of the Tractate in such a strict and tight manner as a

95

sonata' and thought of *The Glass Bead Game* as having the form of a fugue.

As an aside—but one having bearing upon Hesse, the 'frustrated' musician—I must point to his attempt at writing an opera which came to naught. As he said, he wanted to do something which he never fully achieved in his own writings, 'to give some high and enchanting meaning to human life'. He noted with tongue in cheek that he gave up finishing the work when he realised that all he intended was already done to perfection in *The Magic Flute*.

No doubt, Hesse shared his attitude of seeing in music the most sublime and least contaminated art form, a heavenly refuge with an older generation of German Romantics. As he expressed it in *Gertrud*, they longed for music as one yearns for a haven, redemption and forgetfulness. Many of his autobiographical figures are musicians or musically inclined. Music in one form or another runs through his books, from Lauscher the violinist to Pablo the saxophonist in *The Steppenwolf* to Josef Knecht in *The Glass Bead Game* where mathematics and music are combined as actual and spiritual accompaniments to the novel (perhaps inspired by Leibniz's dictum that music is a hidden arithmetic exercise of the soul). *The Steppenwolf* is permeated with a whole range of laughter deriving from Mozart in the form of a laughter of relief and ecstasy. And does not Josef Knecht explain how the musician becomes a bringer of light, adding joy and brightness on earth, how his work 'shares in the cheerful serenity of the gods and the stars . . .' and how he gives us 'a drop of pure light, eternal cheerfulness'.

An essential part of Hesse's development was the change in his attitude towards and feeling for music from Romantic emotionalism to classical harmony, from Chopin to Mozart and Bach, from the Dionysian to the Apollonian. On his way to himself through a severe crisis, Hesse discovered that 'the purely sensuous dynamics' of music were not sufficient in themselves. He liberated himself from the merely romantic image of music as a means of escape and a source of passionate inspiration. In his later years he came to idealise the strict mathematical discipline in music as a symbol of order, as faith in the harmonisation of life's discords, as the affirmation of life and its serene gaiety. Hesse seemed to have strongly believed in what he made Harry Haller say that 'there is the immortal music that lives on even when it is not actually being played'. When the Steppenwolf at the very end of the novel alludes to the hope that Mozart was waiting for him, I am certain that Hesse knew that Mozart would be waiting for him somewhere at the gate to wherever it may lead, the score of *The Magic Flute* in his hands.

Goethe's 'Zwei Seelen wohnen, ach, in meiner Brust' must be paraphrased by alluding at least to three souls living, alas, in Hesse's breast : that of the poet because he was born one and craved to be one since he was thirteen; that of a musician because he could not tear music out of his heart; and also that of the painter because painting became 'something very necessary, fortunate, and beautiful' for him.

The musician gave emotional sustenance to the writer who, on the other hand, was also supported by the painter through the growing awareness of form and colour. However, Hesse realised how strong the struggle was between the painter and musician in himself, and this struggle found its way most notably into his novella,

97

Klingsor's Last Summer. Klingsor, the lustful painter whose creative potency flowers as much as his physical power, who burns his candle at both ends, tries to use music to liberate himself from the naturalism of colour, while the colour should help arrest the burst of music.

Another of those mythical figures out of Hesse's gallery of self-portraits was the painter Veraguth in *Rosshalde*. Hesse recreated himself in this character at the age of thirty-seven, as if he had known that one day he would feel compelled to paint. The novel deals with the estrangement of two people, reflecting Hesse's first marriage, but essentially it is a book about the struggle of an artist with his loneliness brought about by his being an artist. Nevertheless, the human being in the painter longs for 'a warm glance and a touch of understanding'.

The kings among the painters, Johannes Veraguth says, are brothers and comrades of nature. There is a strong interrelation between our poet-painter and nature, and one cannot speak of Hesse, the painter, without having looked with Hesse's eyes and feelings at nature. In his first novel, Peter Camenzind expresses the wish to write a great work, 'in order to bring today's man closer to the magnificence of silent nature and to make him love it'.

Love is not only the key word for creativity, as far as Hesse was concerned, it is quintessential to an understanding and penetration of the wonders of nature. More often than not, Hesse saw the world as full of chaotic images, as chaotic as his inner world seemed to him. There was always the existential question of futility, of sense and meaning of life in a decaying, disintegrating world. Only nature has always been the one guiding experience for Hesse, providing a whisper of hope, a symbol of faith, a pointing and a helping hand. But the way of self-liberation cannot be accomplished by deciphering the secrets of nature, but by finding a deeper insight in nature.

Growing insight seemingly relates to some extent to magic. Beyond thunder and wind nature has a beautiful voice, it speaks in a thousand different ways. We can only hear nature if it finds an echo in the inner voice of one's self. We must become attuned to nature. Hesse felt that through the magic experience of nature, through the quick grasping of the inexplicable, of the miracle behind colours and shape, we will be closest to the phenomenon of nature. For Hesse, the ability to embrace nature lies in transcending the reality of the obvious gap between mysticism and innocence. In his earlier days he thought that the secret lay in listening to the pulsebeat of the earth. What Hesse expects from us and what he tried to follow through was to live in full awareness as a part of the whole of existence.

In his *Brief Autobiography* he said, 'I often see and sense the outside world connected with my withinness in a state of harmony which I must call magic.' The harmony between 'without' and 'within,' the secret of the eternal truths and the meaningfulness of meaning run like a thread through his entire work. Through the inter-relation between the 'without' and the 'within' Hesse thought he had perceived how nature reflects the inner world of man. 'What is outside is inside,' he said. The fulfilment of the human being is helped by visualising and realising the unique manifestations of the eternal flow and the intrinsic growth of everything without, of the mysterious 'unknown power' that relates man to clouds, a girl to a tree, our senses to the 'heartbeat of nature'. This everlasting play of interchange and interdependence, involving man and nature, magically opens many avenues for knowledge and love. There is an unlimited interchange of all senses. Hesse's Klingsor 'saw sounds, heard colours'. To find the revelation of nature's secrets was Hesse's answer to the ambiguities of an over-mechanised and over-intellectualised life in the twentieth century.

The imagery of certain aspects of nature had more scope and significance for Hesse's philosophy of life than others. The garden, and in particular the garden of his childhood, was one of the principal symbols. His thoughts returned to it time and again as if riveted to this point in his early past with which he connected the growth of his own being and extended it to a general state of innocent happiness and harmony. Unconsciously, the garden is equated with all beginning and safety (i.e., paradise), with a dream of beauty (i.e., motherly warmth). The garden is a secret playground and, in all its mysteriousness, it is the world of Eve, the place of origin.

There would be no garden without a tree. The tree means a great deal and many different things to Hesse. Goldmund takes his leave from a chestnut tree when he departs from the monastery and, later recalling this scene, he 'saw the beautiful chestnut tree and felt as if looking at a lost home from an endless remoteness and void'. The tree has intrinsic meaning to Goldmund as the source of life. In fact, the tree becomes a mother symbol when he visualises it as having 'big breasts' or that 'her round crown hung gently over the path' or that 'Goldmund touched gently the trunk of the tree'. What innocent and yet knowing love hides behind these descriptions!

The tree's significance reached from the obvious symbol of being the tree of life to being a metaphor for growth and self-realisation. Was not man's path through life like 'Adam's wanderings from the tree of knowledge to the tree of life?' The tree gives protection to man and invites him to be in awe of its miracle of growth and endurance. In the learning process of creating a oneness with nature, Hesse could listen to the message of the tree, as he gave us to understand in his sketch on *Trees*: 'Trees have always been for me the most convincing preachers.'

Beyond the intuitive feelings and imaginings there is the physical contact with the tree, the sensation of touch which, to Hesse's heroes, can convey a feeling of total involvement with the tree. The sensation aroused through touching a tree can lead from the sensuous to the sensual. Goldmund's dream experiences show him leaning against a tree and, in caressing it, he could feel between trunk and branch a wisp of dishevelled hair 'as if it were hair in the pit of the arm'.

The mother figure is apostrophised in a variety of symbols in Hesse's work, but the tree stands for the mother of all creation. There are trees which 'bear their buds and flowers and scars freely and openly and, may they mean joy or woe, they submitted to the great will'. Every hour and every phase of man's life is reflected in the tree, it is the measure of all things. Music, as he once wrote, often appeared to him as 'a living tree', and was the subtlest and most sensuous experience for Hermann Hesse. On the other hand, when he thinks of life unfolding, Hesse's descriptive language symbolically involves the tree. Josef Knecht realizes: 'If he [the Castalian] has an awareness of the foundation of his existence, then he knows he belongs to a living organism like a leaf, a flower, branch or root . . .'

Trees lead to woods which not only hide dangers in

the dark, the mysterious unknown, they also hold a promise of magic and the treasures of enchantment. The treasures are, of course, not real, but an image beyond all reality, because the treasure is the finding of oneself. Man has to go through solitude and often labyrinthine ways in mysterious woods before reaching a clearing, or self-awareness. Birds are the carriers of freedom and a symbol for man's desire to reach above and beyond, knowing of no limitation in time and space. Leo in *The Journey to the East* understands the language of the birds whose sound communication is another key to the understanding of nature.

It is a fascinating phenomenon that nature plays such an active and well integrated part in Hesse's stories. His characters react to nature and respond to its challenges in nature's dual function as antagonist and all-embracing protector. Nature heals and admonishes, comforts and rejects, it opens the gate to its own mystery without ever getting tired of withholding its ultimate secret.

To listen to the melody of a book or river is like listening to the music of life, but, on another occasion, it is like participating in 'the melody of eternity'. Again and again the musical theme of the water is varied: a fountain has a different sound from that of a river; the powerful drumbeats of a waterfall are remote in their melodic motifs from the orchestral symphonic rhythms of the sea. But all these nuances flow into the one manifestation, the eternal voice, and all water, being change itself, is ever-flowing and unchangeable.

Of all the stories and heroes involved in the symbolism of water, *Siddhartha* is a prime example. Water can reflect the sadder aspects of man's soul. When Siddhartha was about to commit suicide, he leaned against a cocoanut tree on the river bank, placed his arm around the trunk and looked down into the green water which flowed beneath him. He looked down and was completely filled with a desire to let himself go and be submerged in the water. A chilly emptiness in the water reflected the terrible emptiness in his soul.

When Siddhartha reawakened to new life,

happily he looked into the flowing river. Never had a river attracted him as much as this one. Never had he found the voice and appearance of flowing water so beautiful. It seemed to him as if the river had something special to tell him, something which he did not know, something which still awaited him. Siddhartha had wanted to drown in this river; the old, tired, despairing Siddhartha was today drowned in it. The new Siddhartha felt a deep love for this flowing water and decided that he would not leave it again so quickly.

Hesse tried to find the answers to the ultimate questions in nature. The symbolism thickens when Siddhartha speaks to the ferryman Vasudeva whose wisdom flows over a few pages, telling us that 'the river knows everything', it can even teach us a secret; namely, 'that there is no such thing as time'. The simile of life being like a river makes us aware that 'Nothing was, nothing will be, everything has reality and presence'.

This can also be said about the clouds which for Hesse have total freedom, can form shapes and paint shades at will, are the master magicians of metamorphoses, they are and are not, and yet exist—even while they seem not to. In *Peter Camenzind* Hesse recognised that clouds are

the eternal symbol of all wandering, of all searching, demanding and longing for being home. And the way they hang between heaven and earth, hesitantly and longingly and stubbornly, so the souls of men are hanging hesitantly and longingly and stubbornly between time and eternity.

In *Klingsor's Last Summer* Hesse exclaimed with the pained fervour of the painter whom he discovered in himself : 'Nature has ten thousand colours, and we have put our mind to it to reduce the scale to twenty'. For about three years by then he had found great satisfaction in painting watercolours. From dabbling in painting —which he started as a means of unconscious therapy during his stay in Berne and his more serious crisis— he developed a passion for it when he moved to Montagnola and the sumptuous southern landscape of the Ticino.

He was always drawn to painting with a secret longing as he was to music. He befriended many painters, and among his friends was the painter Louis Moilliet who had great influence on him and whom he immortalised in *Klingsor's Last Summer* as Louis the Cruel, the Bird, the Carefree. From Hesse's *Brief Autobiography* we learn that painting had its redeeming effects on him :

> One day I discovered a totally new joy. I was already forty years old when I started to paint. Not that I thought of myself as a painter or that I wanted to become one. But to paint is wonderful, it makes me gayer and more tolerant. One has red and blue fingers afterwards and not black fingers as from writing . . .

His friends eyed his new preoccupation with as much delight as suspicion, fearing that painting may steal precious time from his writings. They did not realise that this was 'something very necessary, fortunate, and beautiful' for him.

He painted watercolours exclusively, many hundreds of them, but some of his drawings—which have a fairytale-like quality reminiscent of the nineteenth-century German romantic painters—testify to his basic gift as a draughtsman. He possessed the tools needed for a painter, and, if he had wanted to, he could easily have worked on perfecting this craft. It is significant that he concentrated on aquarelles which need neither a studio nor long labour. Many of them were executed during his walks through the landscape. Water-colours need a quick visual reaction matching the eye's perceptions with the colour's choice. These paintings little tolerate the painter's painstaking attempts at painting an image over and over again as one can so easily do with oil.

While stopping to look at the landscape and immersing himself in its beauty, an aquarelle was done. Bruno Hesse told me that on certain days his father would turn out three or four watercolours, on other days only one. Painting, it seems, helped him restore a balance between the simplicity of an emotional expression and the complexity of intellect. His paintings were the colourful pages of a compulsive diarist, paintings taking their place alongside to his poems and expressing with them a day's mood. These pictures have the same disarming simplicity as most of his poems.

His aquarelles reflect an immediate sense reaction to the nature surrounding him. He was least interested in the reality of the things he saw and most in the heightened sensation which colour and shape conveyed to him : '. . . When I paint, the trees have faces and the houses laugh or dance or cry, but most of the time one cannot recognise whether the tree is a pear-tree or a chestnut-tree.'

He would give away his aquarelles by the dozen, although never to one of his painter friends. In his essay, *Aquarelle*, he admitted :

I am not a good painter, I am a dilettante, but there is not a single human being in this wide valley who so well knows and loves as I do, observes and sees anew year after year and memorises in his heart and lives with the folds of the hills, the shapes of the shores, the wayward walks through the green.

It was not only his awareness that he was not professional enough as a craftsman that kept him from figure drawing. There was no urge in him to do so. The painting of trees and plants, hills and houses in a landscape was all he needed to put on paper. Moreover, he was so sure in drawing the contours of human beings, in colouring the complexities of their thoughts and feelings in his stories and novels that figure painting would have been rejected by the writer as an intrusion of the painter. In seeking a harmonious totality, he neatly—and probably quite unconsciously—compartmentalised the channels and tools of his creative powers. Nature was something personalised to him, something real and functional on the highest spiritual level.

IN THE LIGHT OF CRITICISM

Versified Diary Notes

Hesse was rich in inner conflicts. One or two contradictions, however, were unique in their implications, though simple in their obviousness. Where he thought to be strongest, namely as a lyricist, he was weakest as a creative writer whose poetic power was most magnificently captured and mastered in his prose. Poetry lay hidden in the cadence of his prose, in its measured flow, in his ability to re-create an atmosphere in a few words, to create the music of a thought-feeling between the lines.

He wrote poetry, or rather lyrics, as someone would write a diary. His poems were bits and pieces of a diary in verse, some easily and some too easily rhymed. They were the result of a very keen self-observation. It was as if he had been listening to the voice of his soul, taking down its dictation. When, in 1942, a collection of all his poems were issued in one volume, 608 poems chronologically set up and taken from nine different books of poems, Hesse described them 'as a confession of what I have loved and done, as a complete delivery of the material without retouching and suppressing anything, as an affirmation of the whole, including all that is wanting and questionable . . .'

We can only admire the courage of a writer who recognised the flaws in a great many of his poems and yet had them pass his censorial eyes to find their way into print. He seemed to have strongly believed in giving his readers a full account of his daily mental activities. His desire to open up was a part of his 'will to absolute truth', to an unconditional surrender to his own ego. With the autobiographical stamp on everything he wrote, his entire being, turned inward as it was, saw in the fulfilment of his self the *raison d'être* of existence. Past, present and future melted into an image of oneness in the view of his inner eye, something as temporary as it was eternal, as solid as uncertain because it was unfathomable. Inwardly he was chaotic beneath a veneer of order, but it was within himself that he discovered time and again the polarity of things, the animal and saint in man, his carnal instinctive drives and pure spirituality, good and evil, the one and the other, and this concept found its way into his novels.

Hesse went through several crises in his life. After having overcome the one in 1916, he could write a year later, 'the Kingdom of God is within you'. He became more explicit in his interpretation of what he really meant: 'I seek and desire a refuge within me, a space or point where there is only the "I", to which the world does not penetrate, where I am alone at home, safer than in mountains and caves, safer and more hidden than in a coffin and grave.'

Perhaps a thought about Goethe, and particularly about Goethe's autobiographical *Wilhelm Meister*, written as early as 1911, must be accepted as one of Hesse's many veiled confessional statements which he had made throughout his life:

In a certain and the highest sense of the word, Goethe has always been a dilettante; to him poetry was not only temple and holy office, not only stage and festive garment; it was to him, the universalist, the most universal organ with which he turned to the outside world in order to express and convey

the wisdom of his withinness, his concept of love experienced
a thousandfold.

Beyond the obvious self-reflection in this statement, it
tells a great deal about the young Hesse and foretells
even more of the mature writer. Everything encapsuled
in this one sentence became the leitmotifs of his later
works, echoed in the magic theatre in *The Steppenwolf*,
in the many facets of the eternal wanderer and seeker,
often joining secret orders, and finally in the Castalian
cult of *The Glass Bead Game* in which the wisdom of
man's withinness reaches a peak of mellowed philosophy,
lying somewhere between East and West but always
detached from the irrelevancies of daily living.

The reference to an idealised and deified dilettantism
remained the key to Hesse's attitude towards his poetry.
Essentially, he was a compulsive versifier—in a higher
sense of the word, I must add, to conform with his own
measure of Goethe. He corroborated this assertion when
he once maintained that 'the writing of bad poems still
makes one happier than the reading of the most beautiful ones'. What better admission of a therapeutic purpose in the writing of poetry can ever be found?

His versified diary notes often have a striking similarity in tone, in their colourful lilt, in the verbal melodic
recreation of his little daily experiences, a fact Hesse
recognised and stated in his concluding (and conclusive)
words to his selected poems, *Die Gedichte* : '. . . in view
of the frighteningly large number of poems which, moreover, bore a great similarity to one another, it was
impossible for me to feel the need for perpetuating that
many.' He saw in one or the other case the weakness of
a poem which, nevertheless, were admitted into his
Gesammelte Gedichte.

The best case in point is a very short piece of writing

that fell into my hands about 1958 as a *Sonderabdruck aus Westermanns Monatsheften* (*Special reprint from Westermann's Monthly*). In it Hesse speaks about his meeting with two poems of his youth, poems he had submitted in 1902 at the age of twenty-five. 'These two poems published in April and September 1903 do not belong to those which are still dear and important to me today. A contemporary critic would presumably refer to them as "Romantic Kitsch!" ' However, at the time they were written he was very serious about them. Now they evoked a gentle and magic feeling of 'dried flowers or a lock of former days kept under glass.' One poem was called 'Bergnacht' ('Night in the Mountain'), the other 'Bootreise' ('Journey on a Boat'). Both can be found in the volume *Die Gedichte*, with the title of the latter poem changed to 'Bootnacht' ('Night on a Boat').

In writing to Alfred Kubin about some of his drawings and comparing Kubin's creative process to the writing technique of the poet, he described the sleepless nights in which a scribbling, playful hand is dedicated to the drawing of letters and versification like a boy who cannot help playing. The motivation and realisation of the poem are brought about by a feeling of weakness and futility, by a need for consolation and a quiet inner happiness. Writing poetry was for Hesse mainly a subconscious process. In putting down a word with which the poet wished to express a subjective feeling limited in scope,

> this word was often accompanied by a warning, by a stream of acoustic, optic, sensuous associations which carry him somewhere else, deviating from the original course. What the final face of the poem distinguishes from a rational text is something unique, not to be repeated again, never quite identical with what the author originally wished it to be,

and exactly this is what one loves about it, knowingly or unconsciously.

Hesse saw a subliminal process in the writing of poetry and felt an uncontrollable force guiding his hand and making it jot down word after word. Considering his total orientation towards 'inwardness' one would assume that he wrote his verses quite instinctively. But in one of his letters he turned against such an assumption. 'I have the misfortune', he once wrote, 'that I always contradict myself.' Since a poem is a matter of form and language, the mind is its main source, he asserted. 'Nothing in the poems of the masters from Pindar to Rilke is written "entirely from feelings", as you call it, but everything is subject to choice and work in strictest concentration and often with painful consideration of traditional laws and forms.'

The bulk of his poetry proves that he must have adhered to both contradictory approaches. Most of his instinctively written verses, subliminal diary notes in the form of rhymes and rhythms, are only of interest because they are a part of Hermann Hesse's life and work. What can be said in their favour is their utterly disarming simplicity as we find it best expressed in folk songs. Like the German 'Volkslieder', most of Hesse's poems derive their images from nature, their motivations from love, and both are extolled. It is their often sentimental and mostly nostalgic feeling which endears them to our ear and heart. Essentially, his poems are the background music to his life, a memorising and recording of imaginary and real experiences.

In his youth Hesse had a particular liking for the poet Nikolaus Lenau (1802–1850) who wrote some of the most beautiful poems of the German language in the tradition of Romantic pessimism. They had a simple beauty and a melody all their own. They were very subjective; and only on occasion did they transcend Lenau's personal problems and melancholy. Many of Hesse's instinctive poems echo Lenau's world of resigned pessimism and his easy rhythms that cry out to be set to music.

Josef Eichendorff's poems with their inimitable tenderness, wanderlust, and homesickness, favourites of many German composers, as well as the fairy-tale tone of Romantic gossamer spun by Eduard Mörike—two other poets of German Romanticism and Lenau's contemporaries—were close to Hesse's heart and mind. Also Hesse's poems have the glaze of nostalgia and yearn for an imaginary flower, they are filled with melodies, particularly when read aloud. Most of them were born to be sung. A great many have the lightness of improvisation (even though he may have written and rewritten them). Some fall apart when one tries to analyse them.

In his poems Hesse is not so much an epigone as a dreamer embracing yesterday and today, knowing that, singing lines on one's lips, one can be old when young and must be young when old (both of which Hermann Hesse was). He was a lyricist whose words were bridges on which past and present met, unashamed of one another.

Hesse's lyrics accomplished the greatest subtleties when neither his eyes nor his heart were as much engaged as his mind, when he forced his thought-feelings into a mould of rhythmic philosophy. Two examples can illustrate this. 'Harte Menschen' ('Hard People') is reaching from the purely intuitive and sensuous tone into an area of logic sequence without abandoning the former completely:

Wie ist euer Blick so hart,
Will alles versteinen,
Ist nicht der kleinste Traum darin,
Ist alles kalte Gegenwart.
Mag denn in eurem Sinn
Gar keine Sonne scheinen?
Und müsset ihr nicht weinen,
Dass ihr nie Kinder wart?

How hard are your eyes,
Turning to stone what they see.
Naught but the icy present lies
In them without the tiniest dream.
That your minds do not seem
To need a bit of sun to be?
That none of you ever cries
That never a child was he?

It is different with the poem 'Philosophie' ('Philosophy') which is bare of any sentiment and with a single thought shining in many brilliant facets, at points unfolding with a sophisticated tongue-in-cheek tone. Even though seemingly personal, this poem reaches out into universal validity:

Vom Unbewussten zum Bewussten,
Von da zurück durch viele Pfade
Zu dem, was unbewusst wir wussten,
Von dort verstossen ohne Gnade
Zum Zweifel, zur Philosophie,
Erreichen wir die ersten Grade
Der Ironie.

Sodann durch emsige Betrachtung,
Durch scharfe Spiegel mannigfalt
Nimmt uns zu frierender Umnachtung
In grausam eiserner Gewalt
Die kühle Luft der Weltverachtung.
Die aber lenkt uns klug zurück
Durch die Erkenntnis schmalen Spalt
Zum bittersüssen Greisenglück
Der Selbstverachtung.

113

From the unconscious into consciousness
and back on many roads, anew
to what, unconsciously, we knew,
exiled from there—how merciless!—
to doubt and to philosophy,
we have then reached the first degree
of irony.

And then through avid contemplation,
through the most limpid mirrors manifold,
we feel the cruel grip, the cold
of a benighted desperation
and plunge into abysmal world-contempt
which leads us, full of cleverness,
through a small crack of wise realisation
to bitter-sweet, to age-old happiness
of self-contempt.

Hesse wrote a short essay on *Schlechte Gedichte* (*Bad Poems*) in which he questioned what good or bad poetry *per se* may be and pleaded with himself, the reader and the world that poems are something too personal to be evaluated. When a poem is born,

> it addresses itself to the poet only, it is his cry, his dream, his contortions, his smile. Who would like to judge the nocturnal dreams of man as to their aesthetic value, and the movements of our hands, our steps and gestures as to their purposefulness?!

Since beautiful poems are often lacking the 'sacred-innocent' function of a poem, bad ones are preferable. The beautiful poem has something professional and dignified about it which reflects the establishment, while a bad poem may be the expression of madness, Hesse argued, and came to this conclusion:

> Sometimes when you get sick of the correct word, you are inclined to smash lanterns and to set temples afire, and then all the 'beautiful' poems, even of the sacred classics, taste a

bit censured, castrated, over-approved, over-tame and stuffy. Then you turn to the bad ones. Then there is no poem really bad enough.

There is, however, as little lasting satisfaction in smashing windows as there is in reading bad poetry. It seemed that Hesse could never clearly decide whose side he was on : that of the good or bad poet. His sense of humour, however, helped him in this essay to the nearest escape route when he concluded : Who needs to read bad poems as long as you can write them yourself?

The Polarities and God

What counts most with Hesse is not so much his writing of poems as *being* a poet and living the poetry of life. It is the ability to sense and experience the poetic itself that enabled him to come close to, if not to penetrate, the thousand and one mysteries of man's existence, to participate in the life of nature, to transcend the ordinariness of daily life. In many ways he embodied what Novalis meant with the dictum that 'the genuine poet is omniscient; he is a real world *in nuce*.'

For Hesse—as he so well analysed and described in *Kurgast (Guest at a Spa)*—life consisted of a constant fluctuation between two poles, of a relentless oscillation between the two cornerstones of existence. He never tired of pointing to the duality of life since he never completely escaped from being pulled from one extreme to the other. On the other hand, he never ceased to recognise the connecting threads in the fabric of life between these often frightening contrasts and to show us the oneness behind the puzzle of diversity.

'Only the thoughts we experience have any value,'

he wrote in *Demian*. In turn, we could say that life is not lived if it is not based on and carried along by a philosophy and motivation. Nothing can exist that is not suspended between the two poles and held invisibly together between light and darkness. In Jungian fashion, Hesse thought about these contrasting poles as something very positive in man, as a means of finding a viable sense of reality or of the self. Hesse realised that we cannot help trying to accept the chaos or multiplicity within our egos as a unified entity and that this self-deception is necessary for our existence. In spite of this realisation, Hesse thought highly of the unity behind all diversity because 'it is not a boring, grey, intellectualised, theoretic entity. It is life itself, full of playfulness, full of pain, full of laughter.'

The totality of man was the goal Hesse strove towards and extolled in most of his writings. He saw in love and poetic awareness the only avenues leading to achieving it. 'The sensual is not a bit better than the spiritual, or vice versa. It is all the same whether you embrace a woman or you write a poem.' Intellectuality, love and creativity are one and the same on a high level of existence. Jung also maintained that nothing is possible without love, and later on more will have to be said about Hesse's notion of interplay between love and creativity.

As far as the polarities are concerned, Hesse visualised the creative act as a unification of a paternal and maternal world, of mind and blood; it may begin in the sensual, he thought, and lead to abstract conclusions, or it may start out with a conceptual idea and end with flesh bleeding. But 'any work of art that is not faked has this provocative, smiling dual face, this male-femaleness, this togetherness of naked drives and pure spirituality'.

The inner world of man, chaotic perhaps but full of multiple possibilities, was the playground of Hesse's creative mind. In *Piktor's Metamorphoses*, an allegorical fable he wrote in 1925, he extolled the chance of change, the countless ways of becoming and being. Hesse admitted that, deep within, he was 'a nomad, not a peasant. I am an admirer of unfaithfulness, of change, of fantasy.' In this fable he made it quite clear that one becomes old and disintegrates when one loses the gift of metamorphosis. At the end of the story, Piktor finally realises that he has the strength to release within him the magic of creation, knowing whatever form he accepts will have to be one that is a whole—at once Man and Woman—similar to the Earth embracing Sun and Moon.

Duality, a state of opposites, runs through all of Hesse's works like a thread of Gordian proportions which no sword can sever and only love can keep united. This so much revered wholeness of so many fragments, of so many opposing loose ends at odds with one another reflects Hesse's split nature. In his major novels he bares his own suffering which results from this condition. His device was the representation of two human beings who, in reality, symbolise the two extreme poles in man. We only have to think of *Demian* and *Sinclair*, *Narcissus* and *Goldmund*, *Siddhartha* and *Govinda*. Essentially, they all personify the two basic opposites: contemplation and action, introversion and extroversion.

Hesse's religious beliefs were predetermined by his parental background and his rebellion against it. His grandfather's pioneering year in India as a Pietist missionary had as much influence on the young Hesse as the enticing and adventure stories, relics, and books related to India and Hindu religion by which he was surrounded as a child ('I have experienced religion in two ways, as a child and grandchild from pious, righteous Protestants and as a reader of Indian revelations . . .'). This was the basis for his dual ties to East and West, but also for his struggle to find a common denominator for both religious philosophies.

A decisive turning point came with Hesse's mental crisis, caused by a nervous breakdown, which resulted in a series of sessions with the Jungian disciple, Dr. Josef B. Lang, in 1916 and 1917. These meetings not only restored his writing power, they also helped him find himself as a man. The systematic analysis of his own self in relation to his *persona* created a reorientation of his beliefs and led on to a new mystic experience. Proof for this rebirth is the novel *Demian*, written in a few weeks in 1917.

It was his first work created immediately after closer acquaintance with Jungian thoughts and is shot through with religious symbolism. In Hesse's novels preceding *Demian*, the heroes are tortured by the question of whether their lives are not wasted, worthless and immoral. In *Demian*, the dualism in man is fully explored for the first time. Hesse re-created himself as Demian *and* Sinclair in an objective fashion. The religious overtones in this novel come from different sources and point into different directions.

In his search for a new belief, Sinclair listens to many teachers until he discovers that the only valid source of real values lies within himself, a thought reiterated by Hesse from then on. (Sinclair realises that there was no other duty for man as a conscious being but 'to seek himself, to become strong within, to grope forward, no matter where the way may lead'). Through Demian and Pistorius—who is no one else but Dr. Lang—Sinclair is introduced to Abraxas, the Supreme Being of the Gnostics, a Faustian deity of good *and* evil.

A great deal in this novel is Christian in an un-Christian manner, with Hesse attempting to re-evaluate Christian ideas. There are similarities in the features of Demian and Nietzsche's Zarathustra. The concept of Cain as a leader and superman is alluded to. To find oneself and to be fully aware of oneself is a Nietzschean notion, repeated in Hesse's hymnic essay *Zarathustra's Return* and the basic theme of *Demian*. Indicative of Hesse's newly oriented religious feeling is Sinclair's final rejection of Pistorius's teachings which, he thought, would only lead to new dogmas and rules. All that Sinclair, i.e. Hesse, searched for was the attainment of inner freedom to be ready for and open to any new experience at any moment.

'One religion is about as good as any other.' Hesse felt he could not belong to any church because each lacks spiritual freedom and each of the denominations considers itself as 'the best, the only right one, regarding all those who are not members as lost and confused'. The product of his journey to India, *Siddhartha*, could easily be misunderstood as a glorification of Buddhism. But as much as he believed in Christianity and not in the Church, he rejected Buddhism with its dogmatic patterns, the Eightfold Path. What Siddhartha glorifies is the solitary, dogged struggle of the man Buddha whose inner vision led him along the path of final fulfilment.

Hesse's favourite concept of dualism was also applied

to his religious feelings. The principle of multiplicity embraces myth and superstition, cults and beliefs, gods and demons, all finding redemption in the crowning focal point : the principle of entity. Hesse felt that no human being who lives his life consciously or is aware of himself as artists ought to be, can commit himself to any one Weltanschauung :

> I, for one, cannot. I never have the desire to be right, I enjoy variety, also concerning opinions and creeds. This keeps me from being a good Christian, for I neither believe that God had one son only, nor that the belief in him can be the only way to him or to blissfulness.

But Hesse is fully aware of how important it is for most people to *belong*, and this is why he avoided making anyone doubt in his own belief. The one who is able to free himself from such ties runs the risk of experiencing a perhaps frightening sense of isolation. If he can endure, he will realise at the end of his road that he had joined an invisible new community, which embraces all nations and all believers. He has then thrown off the yoke of dogmas, transcended all national borders. He has united the spirit of all times, nations and languages. Hesse expressed the feeling in his story, *The Journey to the East* : '. . . our goal was not only the East, or rather the East was not only a country and something geographical, but it was the home and youth of the soul, it was everywhere and nowhere, it was the union of all times.'

It may seem incidental—but is very symbolic in this context—that Hesse liked to build and watch the bonfires in his garden. He officiated at the daily ceremony like a priest. In the idyll, *Hours in the Garden*, Hesse described with great delight his daily routine in piling up the accumulated leaves and dry twigs, preparing them to be burned. 'For me', he explained, 'fire signifies an alchemistic-symbolic cult in the service of the divinity: the retransformation of multiplicity into the One.' Such a fire, of course, has nothing of its destructive connotation, it has the mystic power of unifying opposites, acting as a cleansing force.

In Hesse's mind West and East meet as if at the crossroads of a dream at the point where his fantasy meets with reality. Life and imagination removed their differences and became reconciled in a spirit of brotherhood and love. As recorded by Miguel Serrano, Hesse said that

> if you can live in fantasy, then you don't need religion, since with fantasy you can understand that after death man is reincorporated in the Universe. Once again I will say that it is not important to know whether there is something beyond this life. What counts is having done the right sort of work; if that is right, then everything else will be all right. The Universe, or Nature, is for me what God is for others.

Hesse varied this thought, bending it towards Jungian concepts, when he stated: 'To die is to go into the Collective Unconscious and lose oneself in order to be transformed into form, pure form.' The primary question for Hesse was that we must deserve to find our way to the Universe. This can only be achieved through serving which, in the final analysis, is doing the right work, the meaningful deed helping us to reach a fulfilled self.

To find onself is the key issue for becoming. The accomplishment of this feat is shown in varied ways from *Demian* to *The Glass Bead Game*. The process leading to this goal has connotations of Eastern philosophy and mainly depends on overcoming one's ego. We can only find ourselves when we not only step beside, but also beyond our being. Devotion and service are signposts

pointing in this direction. Hesse remained aware that
Eastern resignation and humility conflict with the
Western cult of personality. The contrasting polarities
can be fused—perhaps synthetically only—through the
contradictions Hesse felt at work in his self. However,
the thought was basic for him that 'he who says no to
himself cannot say yes to God.' Hesse rediscovered in
his own fashion the proven formula that you must love
yourself to be able to love and that through your inner
freedom you may find freedom and lightness on your
way to God.

There is no 'either/or' in any of the concepts, but a
constant process of unification of opposites. And more
often than not, it is a perpetual becoming, a growing
while blending many parts, a constant weaving of a
life's tapestry. Since Hesse's life is an open book we can
follow the steps of his beliefs. Such a self-willed, indeed,
obstinate boy as the young Hesse could not help but
revolt against Christianity, surrounded as he was by the
strict and constricting rules of a Pietism that took the
evil in man for granted and was ready to exorcise it with
all possible means for the sake of the soul's salvation.
At times, Hesse thought of himself as a freethinker, but
then he was one of the most pious free-thinkers. In his
Romantic escape to mother nature, he turned to
pantheism, vaguely Spinozistic, with a touch of the
Upanishads of India. From there he came into contact
with theosophy as early as in his novel *Gertrud* and in
some of his essays written in the early 1920's. This led to
his immersion in Eastern religions and philosophies,
from India to China. (Were his thoughts about the
polarities not strengthened by the words of Lao Tse?
'The totality is the great secret./ It is one—twofold/ in
appearance only: twofold contrast.') But wherever

Hesse encountered any dogmatic restraint imposed on the individual, he withdrew. He selected from each doctrine those features which respected the inner freedom of man, the humane and enlightening pathways leading to our experience of God.

One can easily find fault with such eclecticism, one can reproach Hesse for his inconstancy and faithlessness in his faith. One can blame him for taking the easy road in attaching himself only to the more attractive features of the creeds and doctrines of East and West. But this easy road was, in fact, strewn with difficulties. In his quest for truth—the truth common to all religions —and the ultimate in inner peace and grace, in wisdom and consolation, he put into practice what he preached : 'You should not yearn for a perfect dogma but for the perfection of yourself. The deity is within you, not in notions and books.' An errant knight, he was in search of a higher power, ready to unveil the veiled deity, to find meaning in existence and sense in destination.

Hesse was often accused of agnosticism and of flirtation with a semi-Oriental mysticism. While holding adamantly to his belief in the polarities, he was blamed for his inability to choose between God and the Devil. As he made clear in his essay, *My Belief*, written in 1931, he never negated the influence of a 'mystic rather than an ecclesiastic Christianity,' and that this influence has always lived in some conflict—without ever having been at war—with 'a more Indian-Asiatic coloured faith whose only dogma is the concept of entity.' He spoke in this essay of his *personal* religion which may often have changed its forms, never suddenly in a sense of conversion, 'but always slowly in a sense of increment and development'. He alluded that life with his *personal* religion had been a constant struggle with his conscience.

He envied the man who can utter his confessions through the hole of a confessional 'instead of exposing them to the irony of solitary self-criticism', or to the printed page and his reading public, he could have added. Hesse made his confession sound unambiguous : 'I have never lived without religion and could not live a single day without it, but I have got along all my life without the Church.'

He seemingly found peace with himself when he wrote *The Glass Bead Game*, when he submitted to obedience, service and meditation as the devices and stages in helping to transform the desires of the ego into something superpersonal. When this final work was written, Hesse had come a long way since the days of his Peter Camenzind. The highest goal and form of human existence were quite different for the young and old Hesse. Together with Camenzind, Hesse thought to recognise and reveal the nature and closeness of God by listening to the pulse beat of the earth. In his older days Hesse knew that fulfilment could only be accomplished when the voice of God, or its echo, could find its realisation in man himself. He had then come to know God better, 'the one spirit unified in itself and above all images and diversities'.

Love and Mother

It is an astounding fact that none of Hesse's principal characters are women. Even in his novel *Gertrud* the central figure is not Gertrud but the crippled musician Kuhn. Hesse's heroes are mirror images of himself. In 1928 he admitted that each main figure he created was 'a new incarnation, a somewhat differently constituted and differentiated verbal embodiment of my own being'. There the complexity begins.

Hesse's dream image of himself was of a hermit-adventurer, a man who wanted to absorb and experience life as Goldmund did who got about in the world, was loved and spoiled by women in the most romantic fashion, receiving more attention than he ever asked for; as his painter Klingsor, who throws himself into the joys of living and creating; as Siddhartha, who does not deny himself any joyful and lustful experience before we realise that his worldly joys are transitional stages preparing him for a higher purpose of existence. But it is always the reflection of Hesse's *alter ego* whose exploits and worldly experiences have the appearance of lyric passivity. Puerilely shy and gentle features are to be found in these characters, a romantic-dreamy tenderness bordering on effeminacy. Basically, their thoughts and feelings are tied to their mother image as the reality of a dream as much as a dream of reality. Hesse's hero is always a man in search of himself. Most often he longs for the complement he sees in the woman who, under the guise of a beloved, is the central figure of his life: the symbol of mother earth, eternally young and motherly mature. He is attracted by the demonic power of Eve and drawn to her Madonna-like features.

In this context it may be necessary to throw light on Hesse's personal relationship to women and love. There is no allusion to it in his *Brief Autobiography* where we might have expected to find it. However, in this essay he speaks a great deal about his inability to come to terms with reality in his work as much as in life. Reality is 'the accident, the refuse of life', it is always there and at best annoying, 'this shabby, always disappointing and empty reality'. It cannot be changed,

THE MAN WHO SOUGHT AND FOUND HIMSELF

and yet we can deny it by proving that we are stronger than reality.

A woman in her real presence is superseded by the dream of the eternal Eve who, in its purest metamorphosis, is the mother image. His shyness and fearfulness of *the* woman, real and possibly close, arose from such idealisation. In his first novel, *Peter Camenzind*, Hesse found the key to his own feelings towards 'the eternal feminine': 'As far as love is concerned I have remained a boy all my life.' 'Zeitlebens' is the German word he uses, that is for the time of his life, and he wrote those words at the age of twenty-seven. In one long paragraph he gives us an exegisis of his relationship to a woman which, after his psychoanalytic treatment, did not change but added greater insight to the unconscious awareness of the young poet:

> For me love for women has always been an act of purifying adoration, a tall flame emerging from my sadness, praying hands reaching out to blue heavens. As if coming from mother and also from my own uncertain feeling I adored women altogether as a strange, beautiful and enigmatic sex, superior to us through their innate beauty and unified being, a species we must consider holy because it is remote from us like stars and blue mountain heights and seems to be closer to God...

This puerile attitude never really changed. There was an incident in his life with someone he called Elisabeth. She was the dream and desire incarnate in the shape of a woman passing by, walking through Hesse's life. She was an unspecified, ideal feminine dream image of the boy who withdraws his trembling hands from unveiling the secret of reality. In a poem about Elisabeth he compared her with a white cloud, beautiful and remote. This cloud comes and goes and lives in the dreams of the dark night.

He never took woman off her pedestal, even though she made him taste as much bitterness as sweetness, and he sometimes saw himself as the painfully comic figure of the duped fool. When he wrote the latter thought in *Camenzind*, it was a literary flourish rather than a deeply felt experience. What really matters was his awe and uncertainty towards women which forced upon him a passive role. Shortly before he married a second time, he wrote a friend : 'Marriage is not really what I desire and I have little talent for it, but life and fate are here stronger than my thoughts and wishes.' This second marriage with Ruth Wenger was of little meaning and short duration.

Hesse married for the first time two years after the death of his mother in 1902. He married Marie Bernoulli, a descendant of the famous Basle family of mathematicians. Marie was nine years older than her husband. Of even greater importance seems to be the fact that some of her features, of face and soul, reminded him of his mother whose name happened to be Marie, too. In the novel, *Rosshalde*, Hesse underlined that the painter Veraguth experiences his marriage to his wife Adele as a grave mistake. Sometime later he must have had second thoughts about his wife's characterisation in *Rosshalde* because he tried to picture her again in *Iris* coloured with motherly feelings and great delicacy, stressing her musicality which, in fact, was a strong tie between Hesse and Marie.

Beyond seeking and seeing in Marie his mother's image again, he, moreover, expected her to be a comrade who would help him entertain his guests and friends. At that time Hesse befriended many painters. Yet Marie was a very withdrawn person whose diffidence had a touch of sickness. She played the piano very well and loved music with great passion (as Hesse's mother did). Hesse admits in *Iris* that

> she was older than he had wished his wife to be. She was very strange, and it would be difficult to live by her side ... She was not strong and well enough and, in particular, could hardly bear parties and festivities. She loved best to live with flowers and singing and perhaps a book in her hand.

Then Hesse tells us how delicate and sensitive she was, so that anything could hurt her and make her cry easily. On the other hand, in her solitude and silence she could blossom and 'he who saw her could feel how difficult it would be to offer anything to this beautiful strange woman and to be of any meaning to her ...'

In spite of having found a mother ideal in Marie, Hesse's development asked for more and different things. True, he was gratified to have proved to Marie (his wife and his mother) that he could establish a bourgeois home with 'playing the violin and writing poems.' He said in his *Brief Autobiography* : '... my relatives and friends who also despaired of me, now gave me friendly smiles. I was victorious ... I had a wife, children, a house and garden ...' Hugo Ball rightly suggested in his biography that it might have been much better for him if he had gone to Paris instead of marrying and thrown himself into the whirlwind of life, into a Bohemian existence in Paris where, at that time, Romanticism and poetic philosophy were held in high esteem.

Even though he had proved to himself and the world that he could build up a bourgeois existence, a great desire for the 'undefinable something' consumed him. A stranger to himself to whom he wanted to come closer, a dreamer who wandered off into the wilderness of his imagination, he finally escaped the narrowness of his peace and journeyed to India, 'simply out of an inner need,' as he wrote.

Towards the end of the World War I the serious mental disturbances of his wife Marie brought his first marriage to a conclusion. Martin, one of his three sons, also suffered from deep depressions which later led to his suicide. The spiritual ordeals which Hesse had to bear in those years before, during and immediately after the war caused his own nervous breakdown and analytic treatment. The novel *Demian*, its immediate result, represented a psychological turning point for him.

As Hugo Ball pointed out, the image of Eve, a focal concept in *Demian*, celebrated the rebirth of its depersonalised 'mother' dream in other Hesse figures. Hesse felt that those who did not have the strength or endurance to find to themselves, for whom self-perfection was no longer an obtainable goal in life, had to find their way back to 'their dissolution, back to mother, God, and the universe'. Only the eternal mother remains, as Thu Fu sings in *Klingsor's Last Summer*, 'from whom we came. Her playful finger writes our names in the fleeting air.'

After *Demian* Hesse's libido found a new focus and became attached to the feminine counterpart within himself. Hermine in *The Steppenwolf* is a perfect example of his female alter ego. 'She was, indeed, like a mother to me ... In between, however, I noticed for moments how beautiful and young she was.' Hermine, the feminine version of Hermann, is both mother and the dream image of himself while Maria is Haller's female comrade teaching him the joys of his body. The narcissistic dualism in Hesse usually presents us with two antagonists, two male counterparts who complement each other, one of whom may have female features. Many women, with the open secret of love, are found around Goldmund,

but they are rather representatives of imagined concep-
tions and female, rather conventional, formulae in
Romantic guise. Perhaps they are a bit too literary.

There are no women in *The Journey to the East*, nor
is there any space for women in the Castalia of *The
Glass Bead Game*. When Hesse was asked by one of his
female readers why no women were in his last novel,
he avoided the issue in his reply (February 1945) when
he tried to explain : 'In my Castalia the reader with
imagination will have to create for himself and imagine
all clever and spiritually superior women from Aspasia
to those of today.' Was there no better answer than the
faint excuse when he also pointed out that ageing poets
do not write about women and love since the reality of
both have become too remote to them? Goethe, at the age
of eighty-three, wrote the line : 'The eternal feminine
draws us upwards!' Essentially, Goethe meant this last
sentence in *Faust II* allegorically—but not without the
whimsical touch of the lover in the ageing poet. Seeing
in the 'eternal feminine' the creative principle drawing
Faust up to the heaven of fulfilment, to the realm of
the Absolute, Goethe prepared the groundwork for
Hesse's concept of love's creative power, one of his
favourite thoughts. No wonder Hesse stood so close to
Goethe, the man and humanist, a fact to which many
of Hesse's essays gratefully testify. I only wonder why
Hesse could not make his argument for excluding women
from Castalia more logically forceful in this letter when
he so often expressed his thoughts and feelings about
the relationship between man and man as well as between
man and woman creatively in his work.

It seems to be close to the truth—if one can speak of
truth in such a case—that Hesse found in Ninon, his

third wife, a mother, lover and friend in a comple-
mentary form which approached perfection. There was
no longer any need to seek such a unified image. *The
Journey to the East* was the immediate result of his third
marriage, a book reflecting his happiness like the playful
flickering of a candle lit on a festive occasion. *The
Glass Bead Game* was the torch which he hoped would
go on burning.

The relationship between one human being and another, the strong dependence of man on man, the growing
feeling and need for friendships in life were of para-
mount importance to him and became a salient feature
in his works. In many of them friendships were created
between men which were carried by an undercurrent of
deep-seated feelings. It would be difficult to draw a clear
line of demarcation between friendship-orientated and
sex-orientated love in Hesse's works. In *Gertrud* he
admitted that 'I dealt with women as if they were
friends.' He forgot to add : and vice versa. His heroes
not only look for the mother in the woman, they also
demand and expect to find a friend. This was what
Hesse looked for in his wife and found in his
third.

Friendship as one aspect of love has a creative power
which gave his characters conflicts but also led to the
greatest possibility of fulfilment. He sometimes sounded
more doubtful about love for the woman as mere woman
which, in his eyes, had the fleeting power of an incan-
descent moment while enslaving the male in his need to
seek and seek without ever finding fulfilment.

Love *per se* plays a vital part in his life and philosophy.
He relates it directly to the function of man's heightened
awareness and total surrender, to the source that sparks
creativity. He goes so far as to say that 'Imagination

and insight are nothing but forms of love.' Love is an almost abstract concept with him, even if he says that 'only love gives some sense to life'. He elaborates on it when referring to contradictions and misunderstandings caused by 'love' which 'alone is alive and valuable' and not the object to which it is attached. I am inclined to think that Hermann Hesse was afraid of love as an instrument in the clumsy hands of imperfect man and feared the suffering of its consequences.

The Long Journey Into the 'Within'

The fate of writers is inconclusive as far as their fame during their lifetime is concerned and this is certainly the case in relation to their posthumous success. In most cases the interest in a writer wanes considerably immediately after his death, and his books accumulate the dust of a quickly passing time. It is very rare that the generation following a writer's demise discovers in him a contemporary. But this is what happened to Hermann Hesse.

It did not happen because his work was ahead of his time; but on the contrary because it disregarded the quick pace with which the world tried to run away from itself. One could imagine Hesse standing almost still, involved in his own complexities and contemplation, while the world, running in circles and 'isms', finally caught up with him.

The young generation discovered an intensely emotional world beneath his calm and philosophical pace. They loved his Romantic and poetic stance with its blatant nostalgia for nature and an undefined past. They did not mind that all this was interwoven with more than a touch of melancholy and a dash of narcissistic sentimentality. All this echoed their escapist feelings. They were with Hesse against the mechanisation and technological madness and bravoed his anti-bourgeois attitude. They were outsiders on the lookout for other outsiders.

At the earlier stages of our psychological age Hesse seemed daring when he admitted to being 'a neurotic and psychopath'. In this later part of the century when not even the primal scream makes anyone turn around and look at the screamer, Hesse's stubbornly autobiographic approach to his writings fell into a familiar pattern of self-revealing literature. Just because Hesse's work is so unashamedly self-reflective, the therapeutic aspect of his *journaux intimes*, which his entire oeuvre could be called, is both disarming and endearing.

Besides his Romantic gestures and beyond his soul's long journeys to a spiritual East and within his self, a new generation listened to the poetic lightness and inner freedom with which Hesse preached the gospel of self-reliance, self-search and self-knowledge. These young people admired his strength to defy the cultural phoniness of his time by walking in the mental nude through the litter of dressed-up mediocrities; they were impressed by the idea of proving man's humanity with love on departmentalised levels, and they approved of Hesse's goal to pacify spirit and body in a common bond without throwing one or the other into bondage. Even those young people, the Jesus freaks, who tried to drown their despair in a new relevance of old beliefs, found a leader in Hesse's aspirations to the sacred wisdom of a Siddhartha.

Having been completely immersed in his own image and inner struggles, Hesse could be criticised for having consciously narrowed the scope of his work, and any analysis must reveal that his work is open for attack on this count. On the other hand, Hesse knew how to use a minor key for a major theme, how to penetrate depths while giving his readers the choice on whatever level they feel ready to follow him.

He can only be understood in the magic light of contrasts. He did not seem to care too much about who read him, but he did about how he was read and understood. He thought that 'a poet should not love his public but should love mankind, the best part of which does not read his writings and yet needs them'. On the other hand, he was convinced that nothing could be achieved by addressing mankind, that progress was only possible when one helped the single individual to his greatest potentiality. 'All my works can be interpreted as a defence (sometimes also an anguished cry) of the individual.'

By keeping the world at a distance, he could remain a detached, but highly amused, observer, however much he may have felt pained by life. As the prototype of an intellectual, he always mistrusted and feared the over-cleverness of man in our time. 'Intellectual realisations are empty.' It is amazing how much he relied on his intuitive perceptions.

> I have no protective weapon against cleverness and a highly cultivated intellectual technique, nor do I have weapons to retort and attack. But I have a feeling for whether there is faith behind someone's speech and writings. With this naive divining-rod I stand the test of my encounters with the philosophies of my time.

In his monkish withdrawal he took great pleasure in being together with friends and enjoyed the gaiety of parties. In his ascetic simplicity he craved for beauty. In *Demian* Pistorius best expressed Hesse's feelings. 'I must always be surrounded by something that gives me a feeling of beauty and holiness, organ music and mystery, symbol and myth, I need all that and cannot let go of it.'

What Hesse considered his dilemma and problem, as stated many times in many variations, were the two voices in the melody of life, the sound and counter-sound, brother, antagonist and antipode, the constant living between two poles, and trying to bring them closer together. He expressed his doubts that he would ever succeed in 'writing down the double-voice of life's melody. Nevertheless, I shall always obey the dark command coming from within and undertake this attempt time and again.'

To be torn between body and spirit man is able to suffer as no other creature, but he is also capable of the highest accomplishments and, above all, of love as a sublime sensation : of love that can trust, believe and hope, of patient love and loving patience. This alone, he felt, can bring us 'closer to a sacred goal'. Perhaps we shall never be able to reach this goal, but Hesse's figures are seekers on the road trying to find the ultimate within the framework of their existence. Hesse was ever ready to denounce the madness of his time, but he was just as ready to reject any solely negative approach as no approach at all.

In the story *Klein and Wagner* there is a moment of awareness in a life of inner torment and Angst : 'Art', Hesse says, 'is nothing else but to see the world in a state of grace, of illumination. Art has to reveal God behind each thing.' He always tried to put up a monument to faith where there were nothing but time-honoured idols. 'This I have always done,' he maintained. 'In *The Steppenwolf* it was Mozart and the immortals and the magic theatre, and in *Demian* and *Siddhartha* the same values have different names.' Hesse was convinced that with faith in what Siddhartha called love and with Harry Haller's belief in the immortals one cannot only live and bear life, but one can also overcome the tribulations of one's time.

What mattered so much to him was to add meaningfulness to existence and beauty to meaningfulness. He rejected the idea of living a life for the sake of mere living, or of loving for the sake of mere loving a woman. He needed the detour of artistic expression—we must not forget that 'all great works of art arise from a state of love!'—he needed the solitary and contemplative pleasure of creating so that he can be content and accept life.

'Genius', he said in one of his letters, 'is power of love, the yearning for devotion.' Assuming that this definition was the result of his intense belief that man's mind can soar only on the wings of the heart, then we are justified in saying that he was one of the rare geniuses of our time. When he indicated that the task of a poet is not merely to show us the way, but, above all, to arouse in us the longing for the indefinite and yet the ultimate in life, then Hermann Hesse was a great poet.

MY MEETING WITH HERMANN HESSE

In writing this brief monograph on the rich work and meaningful life of Hermann Hesse—both closely interrelated in their often puzzling inwardness and convincing manifestations—I have not intended to jump on the bandwagon of his popularity which began to roll in the 1960's beyond all expectation. I did it to pay back an old debt which I owed Hesse since my youth.

Hesse's writings have made me suffer with him and see life with him in its many-faceted glory. His work made me believe in him, in myself and man the way he expressed it in one of his letters : 'I believe in man as in a wonderful possibility.' I learned to look around me with different eyes, to accept the magnificence and cruelty of nature and man with wonder and incredulity. Above all, Hesse gave me a greater understanding of that feeling of awe for all being and for the brief moments of beauty and peace in a terrifying world which, together with him, I saw growing more terrifying each day.

Whenever I read one of his books I had the strange sensation of walking in my loneliness hand in hand with him who was so much older and knew so much more about solitude. I often saw myself walking on a seemingly endless road, but, in a remote distance, I fancied I could see his silhouette beckoning.

It was in the late summer of the year 1931 when I bought his then recently published novel, *Narziss und Goldmund*. I took it with me on the train that brought me from Vienna to Lugano. While reading it there, I went to Montagnola, to the Casa Camuzzi, where I was told that Hesse had moved to a newly-built house, the Casa Bodmer, given to him for his lifetime by his friend and patron Hans C. Bodmer. I was too shy and fearful to disturb him then and went back to Lugano that early afternoon. I sat in the Municipal Garden, next to the statue of Socrates, where I finished reading *Narziss und Goldmund*. I still remember it as if it had been yesterday. (I can even remember the flowers in the garden.) When I had reached the last page of the novel, I turned back to the first and started all over. Later in the afternoon I caught myself dreaming over a page. I took a piece of paper out of my pocket and wrote a poem on the beauty of Lugano. It was late in summer, but I called my paean: *'Frühling in Lugano'* ('Spring in Lugano'). I don't know how much this sudden thought of spring had to do with the novel, with Hesse and his belief that every death is in itself the beginning of a rebirth.

My planned meeting with Hesse several years later never took place. He wrote he felt too ill to see me and asked to be forgiven. It was the time when Hesse answered a potential visitor that should he really come he would find a note on Hesse's door:

Words of Meng Hsiä

From the Old Chinese

If someone gets old and has done his share, he has the right to befriend himself with death in solitude.

He no longer needs to be with men. He knows them, he has seen enough of them. What he needs is quietude.

It is not becoming to visit such a man, nor to address him, nor to torture him with chitchat.

It is becoming to pass by his place as if no one was living there.

When I received Hesse's little card with the wish not to disturb his solitude, I found myself nevertheless walking up to his Casa one day, only to look at it and the garden in which he often walked. I did not see the words of the old Chinese, but a short line: 'Bitte, keine Besuche.' ('No visitors, please'.) I was later told that one of his visitors heeding this plea was also Thomas Mann, who was said to have written on the sign with pencil: 'Well, then, some other time. Yours, Thomas Mann.'

I had not come to disturb his solitude in waiting for death. Quite unconsciously, I had walked up to the house to be as near to him as I could. I had the same feeling then as if I were looking at the photograph of someone dear to me whose face is far removed by time and space and yet intimately close. It still is.

Life consists of many farewells. Some of them last a lifetime. This book is one of them.

SELECT BIBLIOGRAPHY

I WORKS BY HESSE

Gesammelte Werke, 12 volumes; Berlin and Frankfurt, Suhrkamp, 1970.

Gesammelte Schriften, 7 volumes; Berlin and Frankfurt, Suhrkamp, 1968.

Gesammelte Briefe 1895–1921; Berlin and Frankfurt, Suhrkamp, 1973.

Wiederbegegnung mit zwei Jugendgedichten. Sonderdruck aus 'Westermanns Monatsheften', no date.

Drei Erzählungen. Nachwort von Max Rychner. Berlin and Frankfurt, Suhrkamp, 1961, Suhrkamp Texte 8.

II WORKS ON HESSE

Ball, Hugo. *Hermann Hesse. Sein Leben und sein Werk* (1927). Fortgeführt von Anni Carlsson und Otto Basler. Zürich: Fretz and Wasmuth Verlag, 1947.

Bettex, Albert. *Hermann Hesse and the Notion of the Full Entity of Man in the Literature of Our Century.* Lecture delivered at the Swiss-American Historical Society, February 1966.

Bode, Helmut, *Hermann Hesse. Variationen über einen Lieblingsdichter.* Frankfurt: Dr. Walter Barbier Verlag, 1948.

Boulby, Mark. *Hermann Hesse. His Mind and Art.* Ithaca, NY: Cornell, 1967.

Buber, Martin. *Hermann Hesses Dienst am Geist.*

Ansprache bei der Hesse-Feier in Stuttgart am 30. Juni 1957. In: Neue deutsche Hefte. Beiträge zur europäischen Gegenwart mit den 'Kritischen Blättern'. Heft 37, August 1957.

Du. Zürich. Schweizerische Monatsschrift. Sonderausgabe: *Hermann Hesse*. February 1953.

Dürr, Werner. *Hermann Hesse. Vom Wesen der Musik in der Dichtung*. Stuttgart. Silberburg Verlag, Werner Jäckh, 1957.

Engel, Otto. *Hermann Hesse. Dichtung und Gedanke*. Stuttgart: Fr. Frommans Verlag, 1947.

Gide, André. *Autumn Leaves*. New York: Philosophical Library, 1950. Preface for a French Translation by Jean Lambert of Hermann Hesse's *Morgenlandfahrt*.

Gontrum, Peter Baer, *Natur- und Dingsymbolik als Ausdruck der inneren Welt Hermann Hesses*. Inaugural Dissertation. München: Verlegt vom Autor, 1958.

Hafner, Gotthilf. *Hermann Hesse. Werk und Leben. Ein Dichterbildnis*. Nürnberg: Verlag Hans Carl, 1954.

Huber, Hans. *Hermann Hesse*. Heidelberg: Carl Pfeffer Verlag, 1948.

Iben, Icko. *Hesse's Humour*. In: Scripta Humanistica Kentuckiensia. Supplement to the Kentucky Foreign Language Quarterly III, 1958.

Koester, Rudolf. *Hermann Hesse-Bibliographie 1963-1972*. Versuch einer Ergänzung. Librarium. Zeitschrift der Schweizerischen Bibliophilen. 15. Jahr, Heft III, December 1972.

Matzig, Dr. Richard B. *Der Dichter und die Zeitstimmung*. Betrachtungen über Hermann Hesses Steppenwolf. St. Gallen: Verlag der Fehr'schen Buchhandlung, 1944.

Mauerhofer, Dr. Hugo. *Die Introversion.* Mit spezieller Berücksichtigung des Dichters Hermann Hesse. Bern und Leipzig : Verlag Paul Haupt, 1929.

Mayer, Gerhart. *Die Begegnungen des Christentums mit den asiatischen Religionen im Werk Hermann Hesses.* Bonn : Ludwig Rohrscheid Verlag, 1956.

Michels, Volker (ed.) *Materialien zu Hermann Hesses Der Steppenwolf.* Berlin und Frankfurt : Suhrkamp Verlag, 1972; *Hermann Hesse. Lektüre für Minuten.* Gedanken aus seinen Büchern und Briefen. Frankfurt : Suhrkamp Verlag, 1971.

Mileck, Joseph. *Hermann Hesse and His Critics.* The Criticism and Bibliography of Half a Century. Chapel Hill, N.C. : University of North Carolina Press, 1958.

Nadler, Käte. *Hermann Hesse. Naturliebe, Menschenliebe, Gottesliebe.* Leipzig : Koehler and Amelang, 1956.

Schmid, Hans Rudolf. *Hermann Hesse.* Frauenfeld und Leipzig : Verlag von Huber and Co., 1928.

Serrano, Miguel. *C.G. Jung and Hermann Hesse.* A Record of Two Friendships. Translated by Frank MacShane. New York : Schocken Books, 1966.

Thürer, Georg. *Hermann Hesse als Maler.* St. Gallen : H. Tschudy and Co., 1957.

Unseld, Siegfried. *Hermann Hesse zum Gedächtnis.* Berlin und Frankfurt : Suhrkamp Verlag, 1962.

Zeller, Bernhard. *Hermann Hesse in Selbstzeugnissen und Bilddokumenten.* Reinbeck bei Hamburg : Rowohlt Taschenbuch Verlag, 1963.

Ziolkowski, Theodore. *Hermann Hesse.* Columbia Essays on Modern Writers. No. 22. New York : Columbia University Press, 1966.

III   HESSE IN ENGLISH TRANSLATION

Demian; tr. W. J. Strachan. London, Owen, 1970;
Panther, 1969.

The Glass Bead Game; tr. Richard and Clara Winston.
Foreword by Theodore Ziolkowski. New York: Holt,
Rinehart & Winston, 1969; London, Cape, 1970.

If the War goes on; tr. R. Mannheim. London, Cape,
1972.

Journey to the East; tr. Hilda Rosner. New York,
Farrar, Straus and Giroux, Inc., 1956, London,
Owen, 1970.

Klingsor's Last Summer; tr. Richard & Clara Winston.
London, Cape, 1971.

Narziss and Goldmund; tr. G. Dunlop. London, Owen,
1970; Penguin Modern Classics, 1971.

Peter Carmenzind; tr. W. J. Strachan. London, Owen,
1970.

Poems; tr. J. Wright, London, Cape, 1971.

The Prodigy; tr. W. J. Strachan. London, Owen 1970.

Rosshalde; tr. R. Mannheim. New York, Farrar, Straus
& Giroux, Inc., 1970. London, Cape, 1971.

Siddhartha; tr. H. Rosner. New York, New Directions
Publishing Corporation, 1951. London, Owen, 1970.

Steppenwolf; tr. B. Creighton. Ed. Walter Sorell.
London, Penguin Modern Classics, 1969.

Wandering; tr. J. Wright. London, Cape, 1972.